MANHATTAN
TO WEST CORK
Alice's Adventures in Ireland

MANHATTAN
TO WEST CORK
Alice's Adventures in Ireland

ALICE CAREY

The Collins Press

FIRST PUBLISHED IN 2016 BY
The Collins Press
West Link Park
Doughcloyne
Wilton
Cork
T12 N5EF
Ireland

A CIP record for this book is available from the British Library.

Paperback ISBN: 978-1-84889-273-6
PDF eBook ISBN: 978-1-84889-575-1
EPUB eBook ISBN: 978-1-84889-576-8
Kindle ISBN: 978-1-84889-577-5

Typesetting by Carrigboy Typesetting Services
Typeset in Sabon
Printed in Malta by Gutenberg Press Limited

Inside cover photographs courtesy Ari Cohen Advanced Style

I dedicate this book to two men: my husband, Geoffrey Knox, and my first friend in west Cork, Ronnie Payne, both of whom care deeply about my writing and me.

I also wish to pay tribute to departed west Cork friends: Vera Brain, antique dealer; Michael J. Carroll, Bantry Bookstore; Marie Donovan, taxi driver; Dennis Hill, Aga man; Sally Johnston, friend; Justin McCarthy, butcher; Malachy McCarthy, Mal's Cabs; and Richard McKenzie, portrait painter.

They would be delighted to hear my tale.

Contents

Long before Geoffrey and Alice restored the Big House, Alice was determined to start a garden. First they planted thirty white rose bushes called Rambling Rector. Here is Alice, about a year later, about to strew her first hundred King Alfred daffodils among them.

I

A Tale of Two Houses

I'm walking back up the lane after placing a Halloween pumpkin on the stone pillar by the road. It will probably be nicked like last year's, but it doesn't matter. What matters is that it's there now to light the way for cars on their way to the village.

Up ahead, around the bend by the willows, I can see the old house on the ridge. In the twilight it doesn't look much different from when I first saw it abandoned and lonely. Yet, what a cavalcade of memory it stirs up in me.

Snapshots of me there, there and there, flutter through my mind like autumn leaves, as I join my hands together in silent applause that eighteen years later I'm still here.

It has gone dark. I approach alone. My husband has placed lit candles in every window. What a long way we both have come.

* * *

It's a blow-winds-and-crack-your-cheeks night in west Cork. The wind is howling off the bay and bouncing off the chimney pots of Bantry House, where Geoffrey and I are the only guests. We have spent the day looking at derelict houses – the kind auctioneers are dying to get rid of – and are now sitting in front of a blazing fire. I'm sipping a double whiskey, hoping it will warm me up, and Geoffrey is nursing a pint.

Spread out on a Chinese lacquered table is a set of Polaroid photos of a nineteenth-century house we are thinking of buying. For it's on a flight of fancy we came over to Cork from New York for a long winter weekend, hoping to fulfill a middle-age dream – buying and restoring a house in Ireland.

It is not blood or my mother's Kerry roots that bring me back. Everyone that once mattered is now dead, including Mammie, as I called her, and Carey, as we both called my father. So I'm more than a bit conflicted when I recall that snowy winter a few years ago with Geoffrey and me on the couch in front of our Manhattan fireplace, thinking about the future.

'So where,' says he, apropos of nothing, 'do you want to be at the end of the century?'

A loaded question considering all the terrible things we'd been through the past ten years. While AIDS relentlessly killed our closest friends one after another, I endured a mysterious, near-fatal illness that mimicked AIDS. I'd recovered; no one else had. So we hadn't thought or spoken about the future, other than that we feared getting older.

On this particulary pretty snowy night, I wanted to keep it light and say 'any old place with you', but I didn't. Instead I said, 'I'd like to live some place other than New York City.'

As the truth tumbled out of my mouth, guilt washed over me at the thought of defection. New Yorkers never admit they'd like to live anywhere but New York. But then, Geoffrey said, 'Me, too,' and in a heartbeat we embraced our destiny.

That whole winter all we talked about were places. Places we visited when we were young. Places we saw in the movies. Places we drooled over in magazines. Places with songs written about them. Then we'd get silly, choose an appropriate CD and sing along.

'Hate California, it's cold and it's damp.' 'We're off on the road to Morocco.' 'I love Paris in the springtime.'

And when we got really revved up, we'd draw up lists of countries to see where we matched.

On the night we chose Ireland, Sinatra was singing.

'The fire will dwindle into glowing ashes, for flame and love will never die.'

Like children writing up Christmas wish lists, our hands shielding our dreams from each other's prying eyes, each of us wrote down Ireland, the first country we visited when we became lovers oh so long ago.

It's now the 1990s, and here we are at Bantry House looking at a shivery set of snaps of a house we're falling in love with. Compulsively, we keep shuffling them around like a deck of cards, hoping they will add clarity to why we want to do this. They don't.

There I am, pointing with glee to a house I can barely see in the dark. There's Geoffrey trying to free a woolly old ram from brambles. There's a sickly calf with its head sticking out of a window in a derelict stable. There's a crumbling fireplace big enough to roast a pig on a spit.

Each snap is grimmer than the next except for the last. The evening sun coming out for a second on a big house on a ridge that looked like the mythic Manderley.

Hours later, Geoffrey is fast asleep and I'm sitting at the window wide awake. The tolling of the clock on the Bantry House battlements ferries me to another island off the coast of Long Island. To a sandbar called Fire Island and a village called Cherry Grove, where for the last twenty years we spent nearly every weekend.

I can see our house shaded by giant pine trees so clearly: our little wooden house we had deserted this Thanksgiving weekend to come to Ireland in search of a stone one. We had come into a little money when both Geoffrey's parents had died in the same year. And in true Irish fashion I wanted a house with land.

I had fallen in love with Cherry Grove long before meeting Geoffrey. I was on my own and a gay neighbour invited me out for the weekend. I had never seen anything like 'the Grove' in my life. Everything was movie beautiful. Everyone was happy. Being on a sandy barrier island way away from New York, there was a Never Never Land quality about the Grove. No cars. Few shops. No sidewalks, just wooden boardwalks. Reached by ferry. Everyone used a sturdy little red Radio Flyer wagon – a four-wheeled trolley with a long handle – to bring stuff to their house; and, of course, the Atlantic where I swam way beyond the breakers every day.

As the Bantry House bell continued to toll, I played my clock game. If it's one in the morning here, it's eight in the evening there. The screen door is open and Geoffrey and I are listening to the sound of the ocean breaking on shore. I can hear it clearly. But it's competing with Mammie's voice playing loudly in my head.

'Alice M'rie, why have ye come back to Ireland if your heart is still back on that island? No matter what places you wrote down on that list, your heart is still there.'

I can see it, 'The Magic Flute', lonely, flowerless, wineless. If we dare buy this house, we'll have to sell it.

She's right, of course Mammie is, about my heart being in one place while my feet are in another. This is an island. That is an island. Why in God's name am I thinking of moving from one island to another?

'Geoffrey, you awake? I can't sleep. I keep thinking of the house …'

'Which house?'

'*Our* house.'

Geoffrey gets up. I can't see him, or he me.

'I'm missing that part of us.'

'What part? I'm here.'

'Us at the house, us in the ocean. Once we leave it'll all be gone. I miss us standing on the top deck, listening to train whistles on Long Island. What will we listen to here in Ireland, in the still of the night?'

Geoffrey puts his arms around me and we start dancing in place, like we often do to give each other comfort. An old song comes into my head and I start to sing quietly, 'In the still of the night, when the world is in slumber …'

Geoffrey interrupts. 'We'll listen to the silence and hear new things.' Just then we hear a foghorn on Bantry Bay.

'See.'

* * *

By 5 a.m. the storm has broken. A pink winter dawn lights up the bay. It's Bantry Fair Day (*our town* as we're starting to call it). Wolfe Tone Square is packed with cars and people; and the two of us are walking around and laughing away so giddily about the idea of buying a house we barely saw in the dark, you would think we were getting it for free.

O'Brien Electric has Gay Byrne booming out to the Square. Seems Taoiseach Albert Reynolds' government is being brought down by old allegations involving an uncensored paedophile priest and altar boys.

We have no idea who Gay is. Yet call-ins are eager to put in their two cents.

'A man of God ... you'd think he'd know better.'

Sure he would. I see my twelve-year-old self, walking down a Killarney street holding hands with Father Bob, my uncle the priest.

Quickly dashing that image into the bay, I focus on Bantry. It's hopping. Geoffrey and I stroll about arm in arm up one street and down the other – streets with charming names like Marino and Old Barrack Road – deeming every chicken, every fish and every olive we see wonderful. Yet our actions, let alone our garb, single us out.

We gawk while everyone else ambles, trading bits of craic. Not that I knew what the word meant at the time. Women with pushchairs cluster in close little groups, sharing the latest news. And I think, how would we, a couple childless by choice, fit in?

A fresh wind has cleared away the clouds covering the surrounding hills to reveal Day-Glo green pastures, dotted with sheep. Keeping our 'wows' to a minimum we continue striding around. Butchers wearing straw hats and blue-striped aprons are laying out trays of lamb cutlets. Regulars stand outside Paddy Power hoping to get lucky. In the Bake House women gossip over 'elevenses', another word unfamiliar to me. And still Gay Byrne's soothing voice echoes from shop to shop with listeners saying ''Tis sad, 'tis sad. A disgrace on the country.' Yet, despite this disturbing news, I like Bantry.

After 'elevenses' ourselves, we drive back for another look at the house. We need a better look, a determining look, an is-it-worth-it-in-the-long-run-and-if-it-is-we'll-bargain-you-down-look, aimed directly at the auctioneer handling the property.

Yesterday, since I'm the one with an Irish accent, I dealt with the bantam rooster behind his desk. When

I said we wanted to restore an *old* house, he informed me that in Ireland an old house is called a Ruin. Then with a withering stare he reached for Binder 3 featuring unsellable properties, and sneering, he pushed it across the desk.

The cute hoor thought he had us pegged when we darkened the door and all he saw were dollar signs. I wanted to scream at him. 'You fool! How can I put into words what I want when I know you're laughing at us *rich* Americans? How dare you be the judge?

'How can I tell you I want a house where the rocks were frosted with moss before Queen Maebh was buried on Knocknarea? A house built long before Joyce wrote one word. A house where walls breathe memories, and fields bear hoof marks of horses long gone.' But I say nothing. Silently, he Xeroxes a page with a picture of a Ruin and tells us to drive towards Kilcrohane.

A herd of cows munching clumps of scraggly grass blocks the surprisingly twisty and deeply rutted path. So we sit in the car listening to Radio Kerry's death notices, while gazing up at a house that has been uninhabited for over sixty years. From a book of place names we have just bought, we learn that the townland of Dromataniheen means 'ridge of the little fox'. But who built that house and why was it abandoned?

Since cows always win, we leave the car where it is and walk past them up the hill. Without keys, we climb through a gaping hole, once a kitchen window, just like we had done the night before.

Thrilled to be standing on an earthen floor in what might become *our* house, we separate out. Geoffrey explores here and me there, just like we do in bookstores, antique malls and salvage yards. Yet even through three-foot-thick stonewalls I can hear his brain clicking away.

'Boy, this is beautiful. No electricity. No plumbing. There's so much to fix and to do it will take years! Look at these stone steps going up to a hayloft! Look at all this land/space/birds/sky/valleys/hills/rocks/mountains/water. This is where I want to spend the rest of my life.'

While I think: 'An Aga here, a shabby-chic sofa there. William Morris wallpaper. Climbing roses over the door. And a cat ... maybe.'

The house is stripped of its furniture. Yet the outlines of a huge dresser in the kitchen and a wardrobe in an upstairs bedroom remain on the walls, as well as a centre sliver of painted carpet on the stairs. Around the windows mildewed plaster drips green ooze.

The house was once wallpapered. So I go around carefully tearing strips of paper that once dressed every room: Blue and pink roses in the boudoir, red Chinoiserie in the box room, grey and red in the parlour. I count the fireplaces. If we clean out all the birds' nests we might get good fires going in the ... one, two, three, four of them.

The day is flying. Tomorrow morning's New York flight looms. Do we make Bantam Rooster an offer? The house that we're starting to call the Big House, with its stable, outbuildings and four acres is only £35,000. *Only*? It seems affordable. But is it practical? Our dream is a dream with consequence.

Night is falling fast as we walk the land, blinking into the twilight. At best it's faded grandeur. At worst it is dereliction. A good distance away from the Big House is a stable and several tumbledown one-roomed stone dwellings clustered around a central courtyard. These are the real ruins.

The darkening evening, the mud, the piles of stones, the sickly calf tethered to a post, is overwhelming to the point of being stifling. Trying to make sense of it all, I call to mind the cover of *The Great Hunger* by Cecil Woodham-Smith, one of the few books we had in New York when I was a child. A book that remained by the telephone unopened and avoided.

Father Bob bought it for me. I can still hear him say – in that way he had of gesturing with his nicotine-stained fingers – that I '*especially* should know about *it*.'

It! My mother and father never said *Famine*. If the subject came up at all, say in the Irish-American newspapers, 'it' was used; and Mammie didn't even say that. She never let on a thing. Neither she nor Carey ever talked about the Famine. Yet they must have felt it in their bones. Their grandparents lived through it, their grandparents who spoke Irish. Then again, hadn't Mammie married Carey to flee Ireland and settle in America? At least that's what I thought. They didn't talk about that either.

The resemblance of *The Great Hunger*'s cover to the spot where I was standing made me feel uncomfortable. Depicted in the Romantic style of nineteenth-century paintings was the image of a barefoot young woman with long black hair, wearing a green shawl, standing alone in the rubble of a one-roomed cottage by the side of the road. Galloping off is a troop of English soldiers who had knocked down her home. The woman is boldly clenching her fist up to heaven.

This cluster of cottages, this clachan of ruined dwellings is the Famine.

This is my bloodline.

It finally hits home.

Now I know why the Careys didn't want anything to do with *it*.

Standing in the rubble of a ruined cottage my imagination goes wild. I'm bolted to the spot. Looking back up at the Big House I am transfixed by the proximity of poor to rich. Moss coating every rock and a few end-of-summer dog roses struggling to survive soften what I see before me. Everything looks beautiful there in the evening light and, at the same time, terrible.

My eye settles upon a small building that, to the romantic in me, resembles a monastic cell or a hermitage. It has a clean-cut rectangular opening so low I have to stoop to enter, and I do. I stand on the remains of a cobbled floor about three feet wide with a gable wall high enough to accom-modate a man well over seven feet tall. Maybe a monk once prayed here. I like that, though I'm sure it isn't so.

On the western edge of the courtyard is a well with very cold water. Not like Snow White's wishing well, but an enclosed spring that I figure must have provided water for the entire clachan of Dromataniheen.

Sadness pulsates the air. I can practically smell it. This is not neutral territory. I am trespassing on a part of Ireland's bloody past, that is my bloody past. Regardless of our good intentions to buy this property and honour the past, I realise I am standing in a place of fierce conflict.

Looking up at the Big House, as Geoffrey and I started calling it, I picture the nineteenth-century Protestant family who lived there, gathering around the hearth on a cool winter night such as this, drinking tea and maybe playing cards. They're warm from the fire and, I'm sure, content. While the Catholics living down here in the gully in this poor clachan haven't a pot to piss in. The marked difference between the Big House and the ravaged huts scattered about make my imagination go wild. Who lived there? Were they related? Did any of them work for whoever lived up in the Big House? Figuring that its owners must have kept horses, Geoffrey and I pick the best of the ruined huts and call it the Stable. Whether it was or wasn't, we'll never know.

As dusk proceeds into evening, my thoughts turn to Mammie. How could they not? I imagine her as a chic young woman, with a 1930s bob, running from Killarney to New York to seek her future. Her dream had always been to own a house. Yet she and Carey had never been able to afford one. Maybe he didn't even want one. I don't know. They never talked about things like that for fear of 'rising above their station'.

Now here I am, considering buying this Big House and the clachan, whilst already owning a house. I hope

Mammie would be happy for me. I doubt it. She'd probably be jealous.

Night falls. Geoffrey and I must decide do we or don't we make an offer to Bantam Rooster. Driving to Bantry House, my mind spins back to when I was a child in New York. When Mammie worked as a maid cleaning other people's houses.

I have to tell the story again. The story of how Mammie became 'Big Alice' and I became 'Little Alice'. Geoffrey has heard this far too much. Yet, I must tell it here in Ireland because my guilt at rising above my station continues to haunt me.

2

Miss D.'s Manse

I'm very young, very small and very pale. It's the late 1950s and I'm standing by a gas cooker with Mammie, in our apartment in Queens, New York. When the phone rings we're stunned. It has just been installed. Carey says it's only for emergencies. So he answers in that phoney voice he likes putting on. 'Hell-ew!'

But the call is not for him. It's an old crony of Mammie's.

'Alice,' says Mary O'Neil, 'are you looking for work? If you are, there's this *thee-atical* woman in the city looking for someone to serve at poker parties.'

Without hesitating, Mammie says yes. Carey begins flying around screaming and banging doors. My cat,

Mitzi, and I flee to my room and lean out the window into the arms of my beautiful cherry tree.

'But D., it'll help.'

She's calling him D. Not Denis. Sometimes she calls him Carey. Sometimes he's called 'the Great D.D.' That's what he calls himself. I never call him anything. I say nothing at all to him.

'Oh it's *thee-aticals* now is it? This isn't good enough f'r ye. Huh ... Huh!'

Carey is running around the apartment. Off go the lights. On go the taps. Darkness and water plunge us into a bottomless pit of fear that you'd think we'd be used to by now. 'But D., Alice M'rie needs ...'

'Alice M'rie needs nothing. She's as bad as ye. Selfish is what she is. Selfish the two of ye.'

Mitzi and I march back into the living room.

'Don't you talk that way to my Mammie!'

'Back talk. Back talk. That's all I get around here. That's what ye've taught her.'

I run into the kitchen and turn on the ceiling light. Carey runs after me, grabs my wrist and slams it against the sink.

'That'll teach ye to turn on the lights.'

Lily McCann, a Belfast woman who lives next door, starts banging the wall. Mitzi crouches under the sink and lashes out at Carey's ankles. Carey kicks Mitzi. Mammie yells at me to go to my room. I don't cry. Worse has happened to me. Worse, I tell you. I grab Mitzi and go to my room.

'Denis, this is why I'm going.'

Carey runs down the stairs and out. *Bang!* goes the door. *Bang!* goes the kettle. That's what Mammie does. Makes tea. Tea solves everything. I come out of my room and hold my tiny wrist under the cold water refusing to cry.

'Mammie, can't I go with you?'

'No.'

That night my Mammie lands herself a job as Miss Jean Dalrymple's maid. My life is never the same.

Miss D. is famous. That's what we call her – Miss D. She's in the gossip columns of all the newspapers. She came from New Jersey. Mammie says she was educated at home. That's why she didn't go to college. But she became one of the first women in the 1940s to produce Broadway shows. She is now the Director of the New York City Center Light Opera Company that is housed in an old mosque right off Broadway. Neither Mammie nor I know what a mosque is.

Mammie starts off by helping out at Miss D.'s weekly poker parties, then a few afternoons a week, then all day.

Carey pretty much stops talking to us, which is a relief. He spends more and more evenings out. By the time he does come home, we're already in bed.

I start going into the city after school to meet Mammie. I've gotten my first glimpse of glamour and I'm mad for it. Over there across the river, beyond the rocks and the rats, over on the other side of an island called Welfare, across from the isle of Manhattan, just a few minutes walk from Park Avenue is a house where everything is lovely.

Everyone calls Mammie Big Alice, though she's not very big at all. They call me Little Alice, not knowing that in Ireland my name is Alice M'rie.

'This house is called a town house,' says Mammie, thrilled to be intoning 'towwwnn house.'

We're sitting in Miss D.'s grey-yellow-blue kitchen. I've just dashed in from school to help Mammie out. That's what I tell old Mrs Ritter who corners me running to the subway.

'I'm going into the city to help my Mammie out.'

'Now you be careful,' says Mrs Ritter, not knowing I'm invincible. Invincible, carrying my copy of the *Reader's Digest*, from whence springs all my knowledge.

Today my job is polishing the silver. An ice bucket proclaims 'To JD With Love And Admiration The Cast of *South Pacific*.' It's so shiny I can see my face on it. Mammie puts on the kettle and I eat my snack. A small can of tuna fish (in oil, not water), for the *pro-teen*. This is special. Tuna fish is special. Mammie says so. They don't eat tuna fish in Ireland.

'This house was bought for Miss D. by José Iturbi, the *pee-nist*. The country house in Connecticut ...' – country house, what a beautiful pairing of words! – 'was bought for Miss D. by Henry Luce, Clare Boothe Luce's husband ...'

'Go on! Husband? That's a sin. Henry's married; and Miss Clare's our Ambassador to the Vatican.'

'Miss D. is no Catholic. It's no sin for her.'

My first lesson in love.

The phone rings. It's ... Zsa Zsa Gabor, Fernando Lamas, Tallulah Bankhead. Unpronounceable names. Un-Irish names. No one in Astoria has names as exotic as these. Zsa Zsa, Fernando and Tallulah are not saint's names and they're none the worst for it.

The more names Mammie adds to her vocabulary, the happier she is. These are names of important people. Saying them properly is Mammie's substitute for The Litanies.

Virgin most venerable
Virgin most prudent

Charles Laughton
Laurence Olivier
José Ferrer
Orson Wells
Betsy von Furstenberg

O Betsy, with your unpronounceable last name and your upturned nose! The nights I spend in bed pushing up my blunt-humped nose with my finger, so it will turn up and say peek-a-boo like yours. O Betsy, how I'd love a name and a nose like yours.

Ever conscious of her Irish accent, Mammie practises enunciating names as she kneels, step by step, polishing the brass guards on the stairs.

As her passion with names grows, my passion for Miss D.'s house takes flight. There isn't a place I don't want to sit in, a window I don't want to look out, or a stairway I don't want to make a grand entrance on. But I must be quiet. Though Miss D. doesn't actually say it, she's uncomfortable around children. She is. Even around me, with my airs. Silent as a ghost, polite as a princess, I am still a child – a child who wants to be Queen of the Castle.

I don't see much of Miss D. at all. I have never been in the same room with her, but I've seen her through the round window in the kitchen door. She's short. She has honey-coloured long hair she wears in a bun. She wears mink all the time. And these funny little hats made of different coloured ribbons that Mammie presses if they get crumpled.

If all Mammie wants is to buy any old house in Astoria, all I want is this one. When I cast my eyes back, East 55th Street between Park and Lexington Avenues looks like a *New Yorker* cover. It's autumn. The domes of the Central Synagogue on the corner are lit up. The flagstones are damp and grey.

I'm wearing my navy uniform and beanie announcing that I am a student of Immaculate Conception School, or as we kids call it, 'the Mac'. My jumper breast pocket holds an ironed handkerchief with yellow roses, a Miss D. cast-off. The voluptuousness of the cloth, squeezed into the tiny pocket, makes me look one breasted, like an Amazon.

I've galloped in. I can make it in twenty minutes from school to brownstone. I have stopped at Gristedes supermarket to go to the butcher's for Mammie. Beef for stew. She'll cook it up for Miss D. and I'll have some too. With tomatoes and peas. Frozen Birds Eye peas, mind you – the best! Not canned.

I walk on the opposite side of the street so I can take in a porcelain cartouche of a bowl of blue-and-white flowers stationed over the front door. I open the door and eye the ivy and latticework wallpaper in the hall. I note the names of Miss D.'s tenants on the doorbells. Gloria Safier, 'The Agent,' Mammie says reverentially. Joe Dexter, the gossip columnist who uses the nom de plume of Cholly Knickerbocker. Mammie's thrilled to bits to have a nodding acquaintance with a man who knows Maureen O'Hara. She pronounces it 'jolly' and he never corrects her.

I put on my little blue maid's uniform and sit on a kitchen stool waiting for my tuna and tea. Mammie never sits. I hope there's a new *Playbill* to look at. But there's no time for lollygagging. I have ice trays to empty into ice buckets and cigarette boxes to fill. And I must do them fast. We've got to get back to Astoria to cook Carey's dinner on time, or risk another night of darkness.

I love keeping Miss D.'s three floors sparkling. I have tasks on each that I do without question. After tea, I head for the living room, step stool in one hand, rag in the other. Over the marble mantelpiece is an Utrillo oil painting of a snowy Eiffel Tower. I have my notebook, and I write down 'you trill oh' so I'll remember how to pronounce it.

After feather-dusting everything in sight, I turn my attention to the objects of my desire: Miss D.'s troop of china cats who preside on the mantelpiece.

'Now, Alice M'rie, don't rearrange the cats. Miss D. likes them the way they are.'

Ha! I think, 'tis I who arranged them in the first place.

Conquering the corner is Shamrocks, a big boy whose emerald rhinestone eyes are the size of bullseyes. Miss D says he's her lucky cat. Next to him is a grey kitten playing with his tail and next to him is a lead-heavy bright blue cat with orange whiskers in a hissing position. I leave him where he is.

Sooner or later Miss D. will give Shamrocks to me. I know she will. She knows I love cats. She wouldn't miss him. She gets stuff all the time. Like the doll in her bedroom – the doll with the white flannel dress, little straw hat and the blue china eyes. Maybe she'll give her to me if …

I'm silent.

I don't knock ice cubes on the floor.

I don't clomp my shoes as I walk.

I stay out of sight when Henry Fonda drops by.

When October rolls round, it's my job to change the slipcovers from the yellow-and-grey stripes of summer to the Prussian blue frolicking shepherds and shepherdesses of winter. I once asked Mammie if she frolicked like this in the fields when she was a girl. She said no.

In the mahogany-red-and-silver dining room there are even more silver boxes to fill with Camels. Match strikers to fill with blue-tip English matches. Ivory candles to place in candelabras.

And when Philip de Witt Ginder, Miss D.'s husband who served in the Second World War and the Korean War is around – the General we call him – I must curtsey.

'Good morning sir, General.'

'Good morning, Little Alice.'

I salute and curtsey at the same time.

The dining room is presided over by a big blue nude oil painting of Miss D.'s back and bum. Bold is what it is. Bold! A 'near occasion of sin'. That much I know. Avert your eyes, Alice M'rie. But I peek. It's interesting. When I have my portrait painted, I'll not have me in blue.

Peeks turn to looks, if not downright stares. I must confess my 'near occasion of sin' to Father Lyons.

'Where did you see this portrait, my child?'

'In *Life* magazine, Father.'

What can I say? I dust a nude picture of the lady who owns the house my Mammie cleans?

And that's only the ground floor. It's nothing compared to Miss D.'s bedroom, the sanctum sanctorum sorely coveted by me, where I'm not allowed to enter unless summoned. Yet, if school's out, I get a glimpse of it through the ritual of breakfast.

At 9.20 a.m. on the nose, Mammie and I ascend the kitchen stairs. Mammie carries a wicker breakfast tray, covered in white linen, containing an offering of Earl Grey tea, wheat toast (dry, crusts cut off), a small blue pitcher of clover honey and freshly squeezed – by hand, mind – grapefruit juice. I carry *The New York Times* and *The Hollywood Reporter*. Miss D.'s still asleep, head to the phone, peignoir thrown asunder. Her mink, a crushed gardenia still pinned to it, tossed on the chaise.

'Lovely day, Miss D.,' says Mammie, her back blocking my presence. Can't let the *chisler* frighten Miss D. so early in the morning.

I take a slow walk around the bed hoping to torture Miss D. with my presence. Think I'm going to break something, do you? Huh? Huh? 'Tis I'm the guardian of your cats.

I take it all in. Drink it up. Furtively. Silently. I'll dream about this for days. Me in that bed, all dolled up in a fluffy bedjacket. Surrounded by bestsellers and scripts. Piles of *Playbill*, a jug of finely sharpened pencils, little vases with pink rosebuds, a push-button phone and dolls, dolls everywhere.

Oh no ... the dolly of my dreams has been moved to a side chair. Maybe Miss D.'s been playing with her. Mammie says all these gifts are from admirers – Carey calls them phonies – admirers, who love Jean Dalrymple, Jean, Jeanie, J.D., and Miss D. to Mammie and me.

I head down the hall to clean the bathroom mirrors. I'm trusted in the bathroom, with its pink cabbage-rose wallpaper and framed photograph of a white cat with a green eye and a blue eye. My Mitzi doesn't match this cat's splendour.

On top of the mirrored vanity, every Elizabeth Arden elixir known to woman stands awaiting the touch of Miss D. Awaiting my touch is the round-as-a-full-moon-mirror, its radiance in disarray from too much dusting of face powder the night before.

Mammie is chatting away to Miss D., who's not saying much.

'The radio says it might shower. Should I call you a car?'

I climb atop the vanity with my polish and rag and kneel in front of the mirror. I must be careful not to tinkle the cut-glass sconces. I spread a layer, smoothly, carefully, evenly, on this 'mirror, mirror on the wall, who is the fairest one of all' mirror, and wait for it to dry.

Miss D. starts in about this dress from Bergdorf's that makes her look short. She is short.

The mirror whitens dry. I take my index finger and carefully, neatly, classily sign my autograph.

Alice Marie Carey
Alice Marie Carey
Alice M'r ...

* * *

'I know, I know,' says Geoffrey, as we pull up to Bantry House. 'But should we buy the house?'

We should. We must. I must bring Mammie back to Ireland in the grandeur I know she craved. From Dublin airport, I call Bantam Rooster and propose £33,000.

'Arrah,' says he in disgust. And he continues on with an expression that to this day I still don't know what it means.

"Ye'll spoil the shit f'r the tar."

I go up a thousand. The whole shebang is ours for £34,000.

3

Alice M'rie's Gay Pal

When I told friends Geoffrey and I had bought an old house in Ireland, shock waves reigned supreme. Everyone grilled me with the same when, where and why.

Old stunned them. Cork stumped them. Dublin is Ireland. Ireland is Dublin. No one had heard of Cork.

Garden perked them up. But when I explained we had four acres of farmland, that *someday* would be gardens, no one got it because New Yorkers have no idea what an acre is.

How often we'd get over here, was met with silence when I said we didn't know yet. Then, trying my best to make a silk purse out of a sow's ear, I'd bring up architecture.

'We didn't buy just any old house, we bought a Ruin. That's what estate agents call these old bangs ... Ruins.' Noticing the occasional slight smile, I'd move on to modern Ireland.

'It's a complicated country ... poverty, drugs, corruption, poor people living in council flats, the middle class living in bungalows – just like in the US. And the Euro is round the corner. Come to think of it, I haven't seen many thatched cottages. Young people starting out prefer new homes with mod cons.'

Oh, did the absence of thatched cottages wound. Nobody wanted to hear this, and I couldn't blame them. Americans want Ireland to be green, sweet and fun. 'Rural tranquillity' as estate agents proclaim in their window write-ups.

Then I'd invoke my one word of clout – Georgian.

'Our house is not *just* a Ruin; it's a ruined Georgian farmhouse.'

With that, everyone's eyes brightened.

* * *

Planning permission took a year. Then it was on to interviewing architects. For the three days we did it rained. Yet our zeal, fortified by a winter's perusal of house books, was boiling hot.

There wasn't a book on Irish houses, grand or artisan, thatched or timbered, cairn or castle that we didn't purchase, devour and scour for ideas. Paperbacks, yellowed with age, were tossed into the bin to make room for Hugh Lander's *House Restorer's Guide, Irish Countryside Buildings, Celtic Style* and more.

Fuelled with ideas and raring to go we came back in in spring to find us a brilliant *man* of vision. (There were no female architects in west Cork at the time.) One who must love old houses, see what we saw in this house, and not bollix the traditional design.

When we got terribly full of ourselves, we wondered if we needed an architect at all. Yet as good as we were with painting and wallpapering, we hadn't a clue how to do other things like put in electrics, plumbing, phone lines and erect cow-proof, sheep-proof, fox-proof fencing. Much less dig a foundation, put in a damp-proof course, lay drainage pipes, build windows, match roof tiles, trusses and floorboards. We knew nothing. That's why we needed an architect.

* * *

For three storm-tossed March days we plodded around in the rain with three different men. Day one wore a grey suit. Day two wore a blue. Day three wore a raincoat.

No one wore a hat, brought along an umbrella or wore wellies.

As we tramped around the grounds it got sillier and sillier. Watching the men struggling to walk in the mud it looked like something out of *Monty Python* and I began to think of the men as the 'three little maids from school'.

Still Carey's voice played in my head. 'Ye need an architect all right. Phony leeches the lot of them, as well as the two of ye.'

Despite this, Geoffrey and I learned a lot about the Big House. Vigorously jumping up and down on the first floor, Grey declared it solid. Blue used a tiny meter to measure the rising damp that we could see for ourselves everywhere. Though it was raining cats and dogs, he deemed the house dry. In a deluge, Raincoat declared the southern side of the house a 'suntrap' – a word unknown to me, but one that seemed promising.

To a man they admired the fireplaces, the size of the windows, the stonework and the cove ceilings. Blue put a smile on my face when he said: 'There was big money here once. The house has detail, pretension even.' Pretension thrilled me. God knows, I'm that to the bone.

Upon leaving each one said either, 'Driving by, I've seen this house up there on the ridge for years.' Or, 'Been driving by for years and never noticed the place at all.'

What no one said (but must have thought) as he dashed to his car, pulling his suit collar up to his ears: 'You must be daft to buy it.'

The unrelenting rain had made us delirious. We hadn't eaten for hours nor had we sat. We didn't even have a place to sit. Yet, as we drove back to Bantry House, with the prospect of a roaring fire and a hot toddy, we came to realise something we hadn't thought of till now: it's one thing to buy a Ruin but it's quite another to have the money to restore it.

But we had come over to choose an architect, and choose one we did. Blue won because he had brought along his dog, and he knew the Latin names of all the trees.

* * *

Back in New York old man Death interrupted, grabbed me by the scruff of the neck and hissed: *Wait a minute! You think you can escape my clutches by returning to the old sod?*

Well, you won't.

Storms will ravage Fire Island.

Another one of your friends will die from AIDS.

And another one did, Geoffrey's best friend and gym buddy, Scott Hudson.

As bad things tend to come in pairs, a furious autumn hurricane stalled in the waters off Fire Island bringing rain and howling winds that destroyed countless houses, dunes and beach. Then, a few months later, a winter ice storm crumbled five houses in a row. In an instant they rolled into the sea and sank. I was on the phone with a pal as he watched the house next to his succumb to nature.

The sub-zero winter sent starving deer deeper into the communities in search of food. At 'Magic Flute' they devoured 200 newly planted spring bulbs, along with lilac buds, hydrangea buds and Sappho, our beautiful rhododendron, the tallest in the Grove.

As Yeats wrote, 'Too long a sacrifice can make a stone of the heart.' That was happening to me. Crusty, mean scabby scars stopped me from screaming out in rage when the phone rang and I'd hear that 'so & so' had finally died. *Finally! Finally!* Pretty soon I began feeling nothing. AIDS did stuff like that.

When I started volunteering at GMHC – Gay Men's Health Crisis – Geoffrey had already become their Director of Communications. I kept a list of everyone I knew who had died of AIDS. When it got to 107 men and one child I stopped counting and crying. By the time Scott died during a blizzard on 1 March – St David's Day – I'd not a tear left to shed.

In a flash of clarity, the kind that can happen when sorrow pries open the portals of the mind, I realised there was no way Geoffrey and I could do justice to doing up the Big House. My dream plan had been to muck out the Big House. Instead I mucked out Scott's apartment.

We knew nothing about doing up a nineteenth-century stone house. Putting dreams aside of doing everything ourselves, we realised the Big House was more than we could handle. Though Blue had drawn up plans for it, it would be wiser to cut our teeth on the stable.

Yet sensible choices doth not happiness make. I'd set my cap on the Big House, and I was disappointed at the prospect of dealing with what I thought of as the lesser project. I tortured myself thinking about how happy we were in 'Magic Flute', knowing full well what was to come – selling up and moving on. When I'd run out of thoughts on that, I'd return to even older days. For you see, Fire Island wasn't the only place I'd ever felt at home.

'*Home*, Alice M'rie.'

When I cast my eyes back I see me running towards Homer Poupart, one of Miss D.'s office boys, the first gay man I ever met.

When my downstair's tasks were finished, I'd climb up the back stairs to be with my playmates, Miss D.'s office boys. Their office had the coldest air conditioner in the world. They were all bachelors. Mammie never called them fairies. All I knew was that Homer and the boys loved me.

It's a hot August Thursday. Miss D. has already left for the country. On the dot of 2 p.m., Homer parades down the back stairs hoping for a bite of tuna and a cup of tea. He's wearing a pink candy-stripe shirt, a violet pussycat bow tie and red suspenders. His greying hair parts floppily in the middle. His teeth buck. Before we see him, we hear him singing.

> *'Here we are,*
> *Christopher Street,*
> *I live in the heart of Greenwich Village.*
> *Life is gayyyyyyyy!*
> *Life is sweet ...'*

'Big Alice, get that kettle going! Attention, Mr and Mrs North America and all the ships at sea. Flash! Flash!'

With his buck teeth, Mammie's name comes out Big Alisshh.

'*Quelle grande surprise*! They're un-dreary-ing Susie and smacking her right up against Master Richard Burton in a *romance de coeur* called *Time Remembered*. No one's ever heard of it, not even Miss D. Without Burton it'd be a flop.' (He meant Susan Strasberg who had starred on Broadway in *The Diary of Anne Frank*.)

'"Susie," I said to her. "Put Anne to bed this instant and embrace glamour."'

'Little Alice dwa-ling, have you read Anne's diary?'

'I've my own diary.'

'Not the same thing. Big Alice, get Doubleday on the phone immediately. Little Alice must read Anne Frank's diary, and Virginia Woolf's, and Cecil Beaton's. Someday I'll tell you what Cecil said to me and where! You know what they say about mad dogs and Englishmen?'

'Mammie, don't. I'll get them from the library.'

'Nonsense! Furthermore ...' (tuna is sputtering from his mouth) 'Susie will co-star with Helen. I told Miss D. that Helen should get the hell out of Nyack and back to Broadway.'

'Helen who?' asks Mammie.

'Helen Hayes! Big Alice, I am shocked. Miss Hayes is very good friends with the Pope. My, this tuna is delish! Big Alice, you do have a way with tuna.'

Lunch over, Homer returns to the Men's Room (as Mammie calls the office), picking his teeth with special goose quills he gets in London.

We start washing mint julep glasses.

'Homer's a sketch. He always wears pink and lives in Greenwich Village. Where's that?'

'Downtown.'

Mammie blasts hot water on glasses so narrow only my hand can fit inside.

'Would you spell that for me now?'

'That's green-witch.'

Homer calls down the banister. 'Little Alice dwa-ling, when you're through, come up for a confab.'

I wash. I scrub. I'm fast as a flea. I shut up about how much I love these glasses decorated with purple elephants and yellow zebras riding a merry-go-round, which Miss D. never uses.

'Don't ore stay your welcome, Alice M'rie.'

I enter an office as grey as a battleship, as brown as a Camel. The lads are huddled over their desks surrounded by a nimbus of smoke. There's John Fernley, Miss D.'s company manager, with that glass eye of his. He scares the daylights out of me. I'd rather be blind with a dog and a stick.

'Is it in straight?' he asks Homer, pointing to his eye.

'As straight as the Yellow Brick Road, dwa-ling.'

But it isn't. It's in crooked. I can't bear looking at him. I'll look at David Powers. He's the Press Rep and he's blonde and cute.

'Hello, David.'

'Hello, Miss Alice. My, aren't you pretty today!'

Homer's at his desk, the big one in front of the air conditioner.

'Little Alice, come over here and let me cool your fevered brow. As I was explaining to my fellow travellers, we need an extra pair of eyes to complete our survey.'

'We need more than that,' snorts big shot Michael Shurtluff. 'We need an escape plan.'

'Ignore her,' says Homer. 'Ignore her.'

Her? A man as smart as Homer should know his pronouns.

'Little Alice, forget what the good nuns teach you. The Bible was written by Daniel Blum.' He waves his hand to a shelf of books with dustjackets in Crayola colours.

'These sacred volumes are called *The Daniel Blum Theatre World*. Each volume represents a year in the theatre. Miss D. is throughout.'

He takes down Volume II, finds a page, and hands it to me to read.

Dalrymple, Jean. Producer. Born September 2nd, 1910 in Morristown, N.J. Married to Major General Philip de Witt Ginder. Starred in Vaudeville.

'We don't mention Vaudeville to Miss D. anymore. Now, dwa-ling, I'll make you a list of names. When you take a break from playing Cinderella, come up here and look them up. Write down what shows they were in, the year, the director, etc., etc., etc., as Yul Brynner says. He's your first name.'

I write down *Yule* Brynner.

'What did he star in?'

'*The King and I*. I saw him on *The Ed Sullivan Show*.'

'Bravo, my dear. I guarantee by the time you're my age, you'll have spent more time with Daniel Blum than with Jesus.'

Going home on the subway I study my list.

'Homer says his name is spelled Y-u-l, not Y-u-l-e.' I put my hand on my hip and buck out my teeth. "Little Alish dwa-ling, shave one, burn the other.' Isn't that a scream? Shave one. Burn the other.'

'Alice M'rie, don't ye be imitating people. Ladies don't do that.'

'Homer's so cute. I love him to bits. He says I must visit him in his *pee-a-dee-tear* in the Village.'

Last stop. It's off to the bakery to pick up Carey's favourite baked custard and on to Deutsch Brothers for pork steaks.

'Homer says when he was a monk he ate no meat.'

'Believe you me, Alice M'rie, Homer was no monk.'

'Is he married then?'

'Not at all.'

'Is he not lonely?'

'Sure, why would he be lonely?'

'Does he have a girlfriend?'

'None I've seen.'

'Homer says the Village is full of *artistes*. I want to be an *artiste* when I grow up so I can live there, too.'

Mammie doesn't say a thing to me, but she talks to the butcher.

'Joe, I want three pork steaks and a silver-tip roast beef for the weekend.'

'Mrs Denis,' as Joe called Mammie, 'you're looking fine this hot evening.'

We walk home in dead silence except for me banging my drum.

'Mammie, if Homer had a girlfriend he'd not have to eat out at night, 'cause she'd cook for him. Right? We must get him a girlfriend.'

Mammie says nothing. She's tired. Carey should help out more. Thinks he's killing himself if he picks up a quart of milk. Slaves are what we are. That's what Mammie says. As we approach the house we see Carey's baldy head hanging out the window hoping to catch a whiff of cool air. It's roasting. We have no air conditioner, not even a fan. Carey says it'd give him a wheeze.

Mammie's key is in the door and I'm still banging my drum.

'But why doesn't Homer have a girlfriend? Doesn't he want one?' Mammie takes the key out of the door, puts the pork steaks down on the stoop and looks me in the eye.

'Alice M'rie, Homer likes men. That's why he doesn't have a girlfriend.'

4

The Cartouche

That summer we rented out 'Magic Flute', which freed us up to come over to west Cork a few times to have on-site meetings with Blue and the builder, an old guy from Glandore by the name of Johnnie K. From that first November look, it took a year and a half to get to the day work began on the stable.

The Keatings, our neighbours, reported that, on the Bantry road, cars were practically careening into ditches at the sight of changes happening up on the ridge. Foxes were seen marching towards Schull searching for another place to hang their hats, while fairies were boarding up their mossy windows in preparation for a visit from the god, Chaos.

Driving up the lane we were greeted by the Seven Dwarfs of Restoration: Happy, Reluctant, Fearful, Suspicious, Wary, Hopeful and Doubtful. But god Chaos held the upper hand. There wasn't a worker in sight. Nor was there a scintilla of charm left to our Ruin.

Scattered around were diggers, electric generators and a cement mixer. Bags and bags of cement, piles of stones removed from the building, piles of sand as tall as the pyramids, and stuff: more stuff than was used to build both buildings in the first place.

Floating down from the Big House came Gay Byrne's familiar voice. Time for 'elevenses'. So we walked up the hill.

Blue and the men had set up a canteen in the scullery. Tea boiled away on a hot plate hooked up to an electric generator. A weak spring fire, fed by twigs and chocolate wrappers glowed in the fireplace. Half-eaten packets of biscuits, milk, a box of Barry's tea and a sack of sugar sat on the mantelpiece next to a jar of Old Time marmalade.

Sitting on milk crates around a broken old table, neatly covered with sheets of the *Irish Independent* were Blue, Johnnie K. and the dog enjoying a cuppa.

And there were Geoffrey and I all decked out in New York black stepping into an *Oirish* situation. Ta-ta-tata!

Trumpets sound for the Lord and Lady of the Manor – 'blow-ins' with money to burn.

'Would ye like a drop?' asks Johnnie K., pointing to a bottle of Paddy on the mantelpiece.

That it was the feast of St Dymphna, patroness of the insane, seemed appropriate. Not only were Geoffrey and I not needed, we seemed to be held in charming contempt. No one breathed a word about our decision to put the Big House on hold. But it must have lost us credibility as serious house restorers. It most certainly lost Johnnie K. money. Restoring the stable would cost less.

For three days we walked around and around looking at everything, as if we understood what was going on. But what really stung was that the stable was no longer ours. It was theirs. We felt useless. There was only so much attention we could give the troop as they proceeded to dig out three feet of earth in preparation for laying down a damp-proof course and screed.

Our main job was paying 'Mr Cash' as Johnnie K. called himself. *Cash*? Cheques not accepted. We weren't prepared for that. Yet at the bank we were never asked for ID. That we had a chequebook with our names on it was identity enough.

The teller would watch me write a cheque for £5,000, then she'd reach into a drawer and take out five packs of rubber-banded notes. She would put them on a scale to see if the five packs *weighed* in at £5,000. Then she would put the five packs in a brown paper bag that we'd hand over to Johnnie K. who would toss it into the boot of his van.

* * *

Long before we ever thought about buying an Irish house, Geoffrey and I became enchanted with the 'painted' Irish furniture featured in Claudia Kinmonth's book, *Irish Country Furniture 1700–1950*.

When I asked around if anyone had any 'painted' furniture we could buy, I was told there once was quite a lot of it. But as Ireland grew more prosperous and store-bought furniture came into fashion, painted furniture was chucked out into a field and burnt.

I thought of the outline of the huge press in the kitchen of the Big House that must have met with the same fate. The thought of it saddened me.

The architect in blue told us that Frank O'Donovan had an emporium full of old painted pieces, if we could follow his directions how to get there. And so we did. Our goal was to hunt it down before it was all destroyed.

As Frank himself put it: 'Locate the large crucifix on the hills above Drimoleague. Drive straight up. Turn left on the windy road, then right again and left at the straight road. When you see a lot of old rubbish, dogs and broken-up cars out in the field in front of an apricot-painted farmhouse, that'll be me and my furniture.'

To us it was Oz.

I had some memory of painted furniture. There were bits and pieces in Carrigeen, a townland outside of Killarney where my mother grew up and where we visited regularly when I was a young girl in the 1960s. The bright colours always caught my eye. Like the lime-green chair in the kitchen that was comforting to sit on, on a rainy day.

Mammie said that houses used to be painted for the Stations – a huge event she'd go on about. She said that tables and chairs, even the house itself, were painted for the occasion. That's why everything gleamed so brightly. The priest said Mass in the West Room. And all the neighbours were invited for this very special event with lots of food that would happen only once in a blue moon.

Frank's Emporium was fabulous. Everywhere we looked heaps of painted furniture lay on the ground in varying degrees of rotted disrepair: hot-pink dressers with aqua trim, faded ochre and red settles, magnolia wardrobes lying next to assorted Victorian bathtubs, sinks and cisterns. All we had to do was separate junk from true dereliction.

After poking around for about a half hour who do we see striding up the lane but Frank, a spiffy man if ever there was one: tweed jacket, cravat, jodhpurs, riding boots and a mobile phone that gave him the distinction of being the first person I saw use a mobile in Ireland.

Frank was a swift talker. 'Oh missus, this is th'real thing. Ye won't get this stuff anywhere at all in the whole of the country but right here in Drimoleague, the heart of west Cork.'

Frank had the eyes of a hawk and a nose as sharp. I caught him watching me running my hand over a glossy cream and lime dresser that, considering it was lying in a pile of silage, was in good condition.

'Missus, ye have th'sharp eye.'

And I did. I even did a bit of bargaining for the dresser, a fleet of chairs in pink, baby blue and red, a wardrobe, a rusted claw-foot bathtub, with original taps indicating HOT, COLD and WASTE and a heavy cupboard painted grey but sporting decorative cross-hatch whittling.

But these were nothing compared to my *pièce de résistance,* a pair of stone lions, each sporting a royal crest. 'Lions?' gasped Geoffrey. 'Lions,' said I. Lions Frank swore came from the bishop's residence in Rosscarbery. Cash exchanged, Frank promised he would keep everything for us till we returned in August.

A week later I presented Johnnie K. with a bottle of Paddy that he placed on the holy shelf while swearing all would be tickety-boo by the time we returned.

* * *

Between sets of 'Magic Flute' renters, Geoffrey and I go out and clean. That done, we walk around the house wondering what we'll do with all our stuff if we sell. Geoffrey looks at the oak panelling, while I look upon a lovingly worn chaise that I know will look fabulous in the Big House.

'Will we take the panelling? It looks better here than it might there. Remember how it barely fitted into the back of that van we barely had money to rent?'

'It's Scott's. We have to take it with us.'

And so it goes. Looking at the panelling, the chaise, the light, the windows, the cherry tree that once filled me with joy, I'm filled with confusion.

'What about Dalrymple's cartouche?'

We go out to the garden where it lies at the bottom of a dune, threaded through with ivy, myrtle and lily of the valley. That it made it here at all is a wonder.

Years earlier while walking on Park Avenue I thought I'd walk by Miss D.'s house to see if it looked the same. But alas, it was now a gutted shell, a breath away from being demolished. Yet, despite the carnage the cartouche remained in place over the front door of a house I used to think of as *mine*. That I'd chanced to come by meant I was destined to save it.

I gave the doorman next door my telephone number. 'Please, if you see anyone in charge, please tell them I want it.'

'Sure, Miss. I'll call you the minute they come with the bulldozers.'

I never heard from him.

The house stood there for months. Rained into. Sunned on. Blown asunder. Every surface Mammie ever wiped. Every window I ever shone. All that was beautiful reduced to rubble. Then one day it was gone. Vanished like Brigadoon to be replaced by a glass high-rise.

I stood on the corner of Park and 55th and gazed across the street to what was now all but a handful of dust. I crossed to stand in the rubble. I had to invoke the beauty of this house where I first learned about Style.

Never, ever again would I be able to walk down my favourite block in New York ('right off Park,' as Mammie loved saying) to try to catch a glimpse of her hurrying down the street, hat on head, gloves on hands.

A gap in the chain-link fence let me slip in. There, propped up in a corner surrounded by bricks and mortar was the cartouche, cracked into two pieces: one big, one small. A blessing. A sign. I had found the Holy Grail.

It was too heavy for me to lift. So I hailed a cab, an old Checker, and asked for help. The Israeli driver picked up the big piece as if it were a biscuit.

'This is nothing,' he said. 'I've just come from kibbutz.'

He got Miss D.'s cartouche, now *my* cartouche, down to the Village. But it was Scott and Geoffrey who got it out to 'Magic Flute' where it settled into the sand and became a part of the landscape.

* * *

On the ferry back Geoffrey wanted to know more about the cartouche, and what it meant to me.

I could see it all so clearly. Homer trotting down the kitchen stairs with big news and Mammie handing him a cuppa.

'Dwa-lings! Flash, flash! Miss D. just sold this house. She's been on the phone all morning trying to find a suitable abode. I don't know what we'll do. If she can't find one, we may have to move in with you and Carey.'

Mammie begins crying and I begin wailing. 'What'll happen to us? Where'll we go? We'll be homeless.'

'Dwa-lings, Miss D. is dying to move. She's been waiting to sell this house for years.'

'But where'll we go?' asks Mammie. 'What'll I do without Gristedes?'

Bang! goes the kettle.

Miss D. calls down the stairs, 'Homer, I need you.'

'In a minute, Jean.'

He calls her Jean! He's never done that in his life. Then, never one to miss a trick, *clack-clacking* down the kitchen stairs comes Miss D. in full cocktail regalia.

'Big Alice, are you all right? There's been such a racket down here.'

Enthusiastic in sorrow, I blurt out, 'Oh Miss D., I wish we didn't have to move. This is my favourite house in the whole wide world.'

'Little Alice, we're moving right across the street from City Center. We'll have a doorman, a handyman. It will be easier for Big Alice, and it's nearer the subway.'

Mammie and I spend the summer packing up boxes for the country and boxes for the smaller apartment. When I have a minute to myself I traipse around touching walls I'll never see again.

The sweet little front room, my favourite, with its fractured mirror and mink throw is disbanded. Mammie says the throw will look lovely on the bottom of Miss D.'s bed in the country. Issues of *Theatre World*, *Life*, *Look* and *Playbill* are boxed and sent to Miss D.'s office in City Center. An auction house takes the piano, and the office boys, all but Homer, are let go. Now it's just him, Mammie, Miss D. and me.

Every day Mammie trots over to the new building to supervise the painters. We're trying to duplicate East 55th Street on West 55th Street on a smaller scale, but it's impossible. This is just an apartment. The other is a house. I pack up all the china cats. Miss D. says she's building a special mantelpiece for them in the new apartment.

The move absorbs Mammie and me, for in some way, it's our move too. Mammie's scared she'll be let go. She's promised a few days' work a month with a playwright pal of Homer's. She hopes if he likes us, he'll take me on as a maid. But it doesn't pan out.

Miss D. holds down the fort in her bedroom right up to the bitter end. Hers is the last room to be dismantled. Mammie goes to Gristedes to say goodbye. They tell her they'll deliver. But Mammie likes to chat with butchers. She'll have to find someplace else.

Then, just when everything starts settling down, our landlord in Astoria says we must get out. He wants the apartment for his son. Carey goes nuts. Says we'll have to go on the dole. Gets into a huge fight. Calls him an 'old hoor', not fit to wipe his boots.

No skin off landlord's nose. He says we've a bare month to get out. I suggest to Mammie that maybe we should go home to Ireland. But that'd be silly. What would we do there?

Every night we read apartment listings in the newspaper. And every night after dinner Carey, Mammie and I look at nearby apartments in Woodside, Jamaica and Sunnyside. They all look alike. Every one on the top floor of a two-family house freshly painted white and stinking of it. None want pets.

'Good,' says Carey.

'But what about Mitzi?'

'Mitzi can go back to the street where she came from.'

Mammie says nothing. She's so ashamed to be standing in an apartment owned by someone not half as cultured as she. Even the view out the back windows hurts her. There are red autumn roses and purple roses of Sharon in every backyard. Yet I see the hurt in her eyes. The flowers belong to the landlord. Once again we'll be renters, not owners.

I hear them in bed at night. 'But D., isn't there any way we could buy something?'

'I tell you, Al, if we had the money we wasted on that one in there, we could. We're broke on account of her.'

I put my good ear to the pillow. The one Carey hasn't recently banged.

By a stroke of luck, Mammie sees an advertisement for an apartment just down the block, nearer the gas tanks and the river. Gus the Greek and his wife Aphrodite are renting their ground floor. We can even sit in the back yard. Mammie offers to hoover the halls and sweep.

'Why, a fine woman like Aphrodite shouldn't be doing that sort of work,' she tells Gus. Hoovering gets the rent down a bit and we're in.

We move by hand, Carey, Mammie and me, lugging beds and chairs across the street and down the block. All the while Carey is entertaining himself by laughing at Gus and the wife.

'Aphro who? A name like that'll keep her out of heaven.'

On our first Sunday we hear Gus padding downstairs. 'Missus, Missus,' he says, holding out a plate of Greek cookies and a little glass of ouzo.

'Old Greek custom, Missus. Always honour the woman. She is goddess of hearth.'

Carey dined out on that for days. 'Ooooozo, ooooozo! Did ye ever hear a t'ing like that in all y'r life?'

We ignore him. It's the nicest thing anyone's done for my Mammie in a long time.

Miss D. finally moved. The street was ugly. The apartment was ugly. Life was never the same again. The cartouche remained over the door of 110 East 55th Street – 'right off Park Avenue'.

'That's why the cartouche has to come to Ireland – to honour Mammie, Miss D. and the lovely house of my dreams.'

5

The West Room

Henry V did not have as detailed a plan for storming Agincourt as Geoffrey and I had for our first summer in Ireland. We were romantically rash. The only things shipped from New York were a Victorian couch from an antique shop in the Village, the chaise from 'Magic Flute', a mattress, hundreds of books and CDs, and a large statue of Our Lady that came from a deconsecrated church.

I was hopping out of my skin with excitement at the prospect of cooking and sleeping and making love in our *Irish* house. *Our house* would be perfect. I knew it. We even gave Johnnie K. an extra week to knit up loose ends and make it so.

Hopes soared as we drove up the lane. The sky was blue. The birds were tweeting. Everything picture perfect – just like in the movies.

A new friend, Ava McKenzie, Fred Astaire's daughter, had dropped off a basket of homegrown spuds, cabbages, tomatoes, artichokes and mushrooms. And from her garden, Granny Sallie Keating had left a dozen fresh eggs and a pot of homemade blackberry jam. Basking in the glow of all this bounty, what could possibly go wrong?

Everything.

An eerie silence had descended. Without workmen the only sound was the wind in the trees and the cows eating grass. Worse, the stable looked more than fiddled with. It was tampered with. In the doing-up, it had lost all character.

As Geoffrey and I stood in the rubble surrounded by our luggage, Tesco shopping bags, a case of wine and an apple green 1930s Twyford's sink just bought in a Dublin salvage yard, it flitted through my mind that in some way we were responsible for this huge mistake.

Interlopers are what we are: interlopers who dared to alter an ethos that had stood firm for hundreds of years. Arrogantly, we thought we could come in 'just like that' and add twentieth-century convenience, while maintaining the integrity of the past.

Then I took hold of myself. Geoffrey and I might be interlopers, but this mess was not our fault. It was the builders – even with that extra week we'd given them.

That summer was particularly dry. The ground was cracked and deeply rutted from tractors and lorries. The stable that once sank alluringly into green slime was now firmly secured on cement and looked like it belonged in Arizona.

We missed the 'old' stable. There was something about it – the whitewash, the grass stains, even the dry dung smears – that had an authenticity the 'new' stable lacked.

Inside wasn't much better. The unpainted cement walls were grey and unwelcoming. A fine film of concrete, plaster and sawdust covered every surface and hung like smoke in the air. Little hillocks of grit piled up in corners looked like mini pyramids. Everywhere I walked, I crunched.

Charm was gone. All the charm we'd fallen in love with and thought would stay forever, now gone forever.

Trudging from kitchen to bath to boot to bed to courtyard, I was in such a state of shock that my mouth dropped open and stayed open. I started to stoop. I stooped for the next nineteen days.

No trace of Johnnie K. and his buckaroos. Were they on holidays? We didn't know. All we knew was they had deserted us. Run off without leaving a phone number. And that wasn't the half of it. There was no electricity, no water and no phone.

Liffey Van packing crates emblazoned with large green shamrocks, were stacked high along every wall. The tightly wrapped sofa was covered in silt. Ken Keating said that when the moving van arrived it was so large it couldn't get up the laneway. He ran the crates *and* sofa up, trip by trip, on his tractor.

The hand of god Chaos was on the hasp of my arse. I began saying 'wow' and I said it all the time. The only thing that worked was the Aga, from which emanated welcoming rays of warmth.

I'd wanted an Aga for years. Though this Aga was the wrong colour (green instead of the requested cream) it soon became my best friend. Niched into the wall like a statue in a church, the Aga saved that day and every other day, and the kettle was never off the hob.

Without a phone we called friends from the phone booth in Bantry, eager to get a New York fix. And of course I said everything was brilliant instead of awful. I sputtered on about *my* Aga. How the Aga man told me to polish its domes with olive oil, just like the cloistered nuns in Galway did. Yet, as with 'ruin' or 'acre' no one knew what an Aga was.

That first night I cooked my first meal on it. It didn't matter that the Aga wasn't turned up to cooking temperature. (I didn't know about turning it up.) And had a gimpy door. (It had been badly reconditioned.) Pork chops took over an hour to cook. What mattered was that I actually cooked an Aga meal.

After dinner, energised with our accomplishment and a little tipsy from wine that we cooled in the well, we started hoovering and wiping. Thus began Round 1 of our nineteen-day ritual of attempting to clean the uncleanable.

A tick before midnight Geoffrey and I, waltzing away what was left of our wits, started unwrapping furniture, fluffing pillows, picking the few wild flowers I could see in the dark and pouring more wine. Yet we still didn't have a bed to sleep in. We hadn't gotten around to lugging an old cast-iron bed frame down from the Big House.

We laid plastic sheeting on the floor, put the mattress, still encased in plastic, atop that and sheets atop that. To the sounds of cows munching grass right outside the window and neighbouring farm dogs barking alarums to each other across the valley, sleep eluded us.

In the morning, and every morning thereafter, we awoke covered in silt. When locals asked how we were getting on, and I mentioned the constant silt, they all said the same thing: 'The house is settlin'.'

We had no water because there was no electricity. Despite the water diviner who'd come in March with a quivering rod to determine where the well should be dug. It struck me as odd that this ancient way of finding water would need electricity to draw it up, not an old-fashioned pump.

Even had we had electricity, there was no place to shower because we hadn't a shower, we had a bathtub. My fault! For years I'd dreamed of a glorious six-foot-long claw-foot Victorian bath, with a tray stocked with every soap and perfumed oil known to Miss D.

No, I'd scream at the mere suggestion of a shower. Showers are modern. If ever there was an eschewer of modernity, happy to grovel at the dusty shrine of authenticity, it was I. Yet how was I to know that silt and dust are best showered off and not sat in a tub of dirty water?

That first night we took whore's baths, that inefficient daubing of face, oxters and netherparts, with well water heated on the Aga, nice in its way – certainly authentic – but not quite enough. Worse, there was no lovemaking that night, nor on any of the eighteen remaining ones. Fie on my vision of Geoffrey and I transforming ourselves into a modern-day Tristan and Isolde, writhing in ecstasy in the Irish countryside. Dust defeated ardour that August.

With neither landline nor mobile, we'd drive to Bantry twice a day, hit the phone booths and call Telecom Éireann.

'Certainly Mr Knox, we'll send someone out straight away in the morning.' But they didn't. They wouldn't. And we knew it. We'd call Johnnie K., get his answering machine and scream, 'We Need Help! Where are you? We don't know what to do! Have you deserted us?' He didn't respond either.

Our one laugh was remembering how Johnnie K. had once silenced Geoffrey, who'd been acting like a little wet hen about God knows what not being completed.

'But we won't have enough time,' whined Geoffrey with a crack in his voice.

'Shure now,' said Johnnie K., 'when God made time, he made plenty of it.'

Every day, desperate to accomplish something, anything, I'd mop the same floor slates over and over again, knowing full well all I was doing was filling the gap of despair with soap and water, because the house was settlin' and silt kept falling down from the ceiling and rafters.

Then we'd get in the car, slam The Beatles into the CD player and head for the local hotel leisure centre to take a shower.

In trying to keep the stable as neat as possible, the West Room of the Big House became the repository of stuff we didn't know what to do with yet. Unopened cargo of our past lives was wheeled up to the Big House, deposited in the West Room and promptly forgotten.

In my Mammie's home, the West Room was special. So special no one darkened its door. Now I had my own. Sometimes, for no reason at all except to carry up a trinket too precious to throw out, I'd arrive with a beaker of tea and sit on an old bench. With western sun flickering on the fireplace, I'd let waves of memory waft over me until I was back in Killarney again.

* * *

'We're home, Alice M'rie.' That's what Mammie says when the car stops at a two-up-two-down bungalow plopped on the side of the road. The view is pretty. The house is not. *Home.* Is this what we saved and saved to see? Smack up against it is what Mammie must be thinking about when she says *home.* Next to the new house is the old thatched cottage where Alice Slattery was born.

It has taken the day to get here from Cobh, and now that we're here, everyone stands around the kitchen with coats on, giving me, her twelve-year-old daughter, the once-over. There are Mammie's brothers: Father Bob, the priest on holiday from his parish in England; and Dave, the farmer. There's Dave's wife, Mary Falvey – never referred to as just Mary, or Mrs Slattery but always Mary Falvey – and their two sons, D.D. and Robert, my cousins. Mary Falvey's just paid me a compliment that's music to Mammie's ears.

'Oh Alice M'rie, ye don't sound like a Yank at all. Ye sound just like ye're mother.'

The turf fire is losing against the damp. The kettle is on the hob and small glasses of whiskey are being passed around. Mammie is in the centre of the room, the centre of attention.

'O Alice, ye've come *home*,' they say, grabbing her hands as if she were a bishop.

The house is plain. It's neither painted nor heated. It has no books. No TV. No magazines. A few scraggly geraniums are in a window. On a kitchen shelf a radio and a portrait of the Sacred Heart vie for attention.

The kitchen serves as the living room. The floor is cement. All living is done here and I've been warned we'll have to use chamber pots, since there's no bathroom. Brack, the sheepdog wanders around, and a small pregnant cat looks like she'll not live to nurse her kittens.

Mammie and her brothers are laughing away.

'Who else is coming *home* this summer?'

'Shure, nothing changes at all here.'

It's early evening and I'm having a ramble about. This will be my home for the next month and I'm stuck. Stuck! I tell you. No walking out to the corner newsstand to check up on the latest magazines in this place. Make the best of it. Offer it up. Mammie is happy, and I'll be happy too.

I traipse from one bedroom to another. They're all alike – bed and a light, bed and a light. At least Mammie and I have a room with a view and two tables to put our stuff on. The downstairs doors are all ajar, except for the room to the left of the front door. Never one for leaving a stone unturned, I open it.

Crack it gently. Slip in. Can't let them hear me in the kitchen. The light from a single window casts a feeble glow on a formal room whose decor doesn't match the rest of the house. Taking up the whole room is a large dining table covered by a linen cloth, and an empty crystal fruit bowl. Around the walls are a few pieces of upholstered furniture, a dresser crammed with what looks to be the good china, and a sideboard crammed with pictures.

Old black-and-white snaps catch my eye. Scattered throughout are Holy Cards – one side with a picture of Mother Mary, the other a passport-sized photo of a person.

I go from woman to man to child to priest to nun as though the people in the pictures were calling out to me. Then it hits me. All these people are dead. They must be dead. They're all wearing clothes from other eras. Do I know any of them? I must know some of them. Some of them look like me.

That woman with a bun on her head and a very big nose must be Mammie's mother, the man in a cap, leaning against a rick of hay, her father. There's her sister, Mollie, a nun, whose name Mammie always prefaces with *poor*, because Mollie died of leukemia. Pushed to the rear are pictures of Mammie and me taken on my First Communion and Confirmation.

There's Mammie and me standing in the street in Astoria before we went into the city to see *My Fair Lady*. I used to think I could die happy, now that I'd seen *My Fair Lady*. There we are all dolled up on our way to Mass. There I am dressed in white for my graduation. There are no pictures at all of Carey. I know I'm trespassing. I'm half blind from the dark and terrified the Slatterys will come in and find me, but I don't care. The power of these pictures holds me in that room.

The only piece of decorative art is a huge, framed lithograph of *The Three Blind Children At The Holy Well* that presides over the sideboard.

Three little girls in rags and tatters are dipping their hands into an old stone well. I just love the way they're looking up to heaven with beatific smiles, eyes closed. It's so spooky it's fabulous.

My eyes are glued to it. It fits in with all the gory fairy tales I love. The ones where girls are blinded or maimed until they're redeemed by true love like my favourite, *The Little Mermaid*. But what's especially wonderful about this picture is that Mammie's and my pictures are propped up right underneath it.

'Alice M'rie, where are ye? Come in for the tea.'

Trembling with excitement, I head back to the kitchen. No one has missed me.

I tell not a soul. It's my secret as well as my ignorance. I don't know why Mammie and I have been lumped in there with the dead, but I love that we are.

I can't wait for my daily peek. When they go out to the cows, I go in for a look. There are the blind girls and there am I, all joined together in a lovely, creepy alliance.

After a week of subterfuge I want to try and wheedle the *why* out of Mammie. We'd be lying in bed at night, she with a book and me with one too. So when I finally broach the subject she doesn't suspect a thing.

'Mammie, you know that room, that room that's closed down there by the front door? Don't they use it at all?'

'Alice M'rie, ye best not be going in there. There'll be time enough for that our last night, when we'll all have dinner there.'

'But why is it closed up?'

'It's for wakes and farewells. They call it the West Room. Long ago they used to say that when people died, their souls headed west so they could live forever with the fairies and stay young forever. That's an old *pishogue* and I don't know if it's at all true. But they put pictures of people who've died in there, so they can look down from heaven and pray for us down here.'

That's all Mammie said. She doesn't say why our photos are there, nor do I ask.

6

Denis & Alice

As we'd yet to buy a post box, I get the chance to chat with my neighbours, Ken and Sheila Keating, when I go down to their house to collect our post. The Keatings fascinate me because they are modern Ireland, not the 'old' Ireland I once knew. They've no idea how they serve as a silent reminder that I am a woman alone – an only child, a motherless child – a woman without children.

The Keatings live their lives in a time-honoured way. It's I who chose to lead my life differently. As Sallie, Ken's mother, commented, when she asked had we children and I said no: 'Ah, then, girl, ye've no one to please but y'rself.'

As I stare at Sheila and her brood of chicks I'm filled with loss. I've lost touch with what it's like to have a mother. Were Mammie alive, she'd be in her nineties. I don't know if I would still call her Mammie. I don't know if she would still call me Alice M'rie. What I do know is, I've not turned out the way she would have wanted.

I've forgotten the sound of her voice. When I try to recall her, I've given her a voice that scolds more than praises. Why, I don't know. I invent her words, spoken from beyond the pale, words that have more than a grain of truth in them.

'Alice M'rie, what have ye done with yourself? Ye ran away from home and moved to Greenwich Village like I ran from Killarney to better myself in America. Now ye wind up in a Ruin ye think you're going to make into a palace.'

Ah well. The difference between the ways the Keating kids are being brought up, and the way I was brought up is huge. They live in the now and the new. Everything seems so normal I think I've wandered into another world when I'm down there.

'Hello, hello, Alice, don't bother with that now,' says Sheila, as I stomp the muck off my wellies outside the back door. 'You see how we are here.' *See!* I see everything sparkling. Ken comes in from the cows, leaving his muddy boots in the hall. The two youngest children, Pinky and Young Ken, start chanting 'Da, Da', beseeching their da to slice a cupcake in half for them.

Taking out a huge pocketknife that must have assisted in many a calf's birth, Ken's large hand cradles a pink iced queen cake. His knife splits it in two, and he gives the iced half to the girl, the cake half to the boy.

The house is silent except for a continuous procession to the fridge. Kids are on the prowl. Open it. Close it. Open it, looking for juice, cheese, crisps, yoghurt, biscuits and chocolate. Our fridge in Astoria never held such bounty. I never opened it except to get milk for the tea.

That the Keating kids are consuming so many empty calories shocks the New Yorker in me. Yet I know my 'child free' standards do not apply here. Patting the dog to centre myself, I see that at least this family sits together in a room, glancing at the telly, not snarling, sad and silent in separate rooms, like Mammie, Carey and me.

The dog is yelping and kids are running around all over the place egging him on. I'd like to talk with them, but I don't know how. Flashes of myself, always with a book, always silent, pop into my head.

As I start to gather up my mail, Ken offers me a queen cake, and gestures for me to sit down again. Nodding his head towards Judy, the eldest girl, he says, 'Well, we've a scholar in the family now.'

Judy smiles shyly, and Ken continues. 'Next year she's graduatin' from school and goin' on to college. I never went that far myself but she is.'

'We're thrilled,' says Sheila. 'We can't wait to celebrate.'

I jump up and hug Judy who seems uncomfortable at my exuberance, so she resumes her place with Phil in front of a TV set to mute and playing *Titanic*. No one's taking any notice of it. The ship's architect is gazing at a clock sliding down a mantelpiece. I recognise him. At least I can talk about this.

'That's my neighbour, Victor Garber. We say hello when I see him walking his dog.' The girls don't note a word I say yet blithely I blather on. 'He acts in musicals too.' The girls are on mute as well.

Bored with the slowly sinking ship, Judy and Phil walk me back to the house. Judy starts jabbering about how her parents are planning to take every Keating in sight to the Bantry Bay Hotel for a Graduation Lunch.

But when I ask where she's planning to go to college, she says she hasn't a clue what she *really* wants to 'do' yet. Though she's somewhat interested in Agri, not a popular major for girls, she says, she's pretty sure she'll be able to get into an Agri college in Limerick.

I'm interested in talking more about this but Judy isn't and she switches to the Graduation Lunch. Plated, not buffet, with three choices – lamb, chicken and duck. She's planning on the duck as 'Mam messes duck up, if she even attempts it at all.'

Up in the stable the girls begin poking around. They eye two prints of bluebirds perched on an apple tree, lying on top of a packing crate and Phil wants to know where I'll hang them. Then after a few more questions, largely centring on what we'll do with all the books, *bo-ring* starts to shine in the girl's eyes, and they leave.

As I watch them skip down the laneway to their own Mammie, I'm filled with envy about that graduation lunch. You'd think it wouldn't bother me – a plated lunch – but it does. I'm pretty sure I got a greeting card from Mammie, but nothing from Carey.

I graduated on a nice day. I'm in a new white dress that looks more First Holy Communion than high school. Carey, Mammie and I are on the subway going into the city to the ceremony. We're silent. That's nothing strange. We three never had much to say to each other. Carey's in his brown suit, Mammie's in her pink dress. They look nice, myself as well, even in that girly dress.

I'd been chosen to be Salutatorian, but I don't remember a thing I said. I doubt the Careys knew what Salutatorian meant, and I doubt I explained it. I remember we didn't 'do' anything special afterward. Back in Astoria, we eat dinner in silence as usual. I want to remember more. But at the same time I dread it.

I do remember the next day. Mammie is with Miss D. Carey is at his job at La Guardia Airport. I'm having a sleep-in. The phone rings. A man says Carey's been in a car accident. He tells me to stay put for more information and hangs up. I call Mammie. She starts crying. I hear Miss D. asking what's wrong.

The General takes over. He wants facts. Wants to know why I didn't get the caller's name. I say I don't know. I make a cup of tea. Phone rings. It's the same man. He says Carey's dead. His car went up in flames on a runway, enveloping him. But before I can get his name, he hangs up. I don't cry. I'm happy to be liberated from Carey's temper and lashing tongue.

I call Mammie. She starts balling about us being left penniless. Homer grabs the phone and tells me to come in immediately. Miss D. yammers at the General to 'do something'. He takes the phone from Homer and I hear him say, 'I'll get to the bottom of this.'

I drink a glass of orange juice. I'm surprisingly calm. I take the subway into the city. But I loiter at Bloomingdale's windows, delaying walking down to Miss D.

The house is abuzz in chaos. The office boys have joined in the rigmarole and are smoking furiously. The General is pouring himself a scotch. Homer is brewing a pot of tea for Mammie. And Miss D. is sitting up in bed, even though it's now past eleven o'clock.

The General pulls me into the hall. Says he thinks it's all a hoax, but doesn't explain why. He was a big shot in the Korean War. He must have good instincts. That's what I figure. He asks me for Carey's telephone number. Then he marches into Miss D.'s bedroom and dials. Carey picks up.

'Denis, we hear you're dead.'

Everyone gathers around.

Homer pours him another scotch.

'Arrah, one of the lads was takin' the piss outta me.'

'The piss?'

'Jokin' … y'know.'

'So Denis, you're all right? We're all worried here … Big Alice, Little Alice, myself …'

'I'm grand. Got to go now.'

Carey hangs up. Peace is restored. No one says a thing. Miss D. gets up. Mammie asks what she's planning on wearing today. The General runs out to his bookie to bet on a horse. Homer and the office boys scurry back to their desks. And I … I get out of there as fast as I can.

That night the three of us did not talk about it. We never did. Years later, it took a boyfriend, an older man, who, when I told him Carey was in the habit of 'doing' funny voices in the street – like barking like a dog – to scare people, surmised that Carey might have faked his own death to scare me.

It made sense then. It still does. Did Carey want to take the piss out of me just because I was graduating and going on to university? Maybe. He never talked about his own schooling. Even if he did attend grammar school, I'm pretty sure he didn't go beyond that.

So then, what did I do on that fine June morning? I walked over to 5th Avenue and took the bus down to Greenwich Village for a walk around. Nothing bad could ever, ever happen here. And for a while I felt happy.

* * *

The bluebirds are all I have left of Mammie, along with her silver letter opener, a sewing basket, a thimble stamped 'Killarney', three fancy hats, a rhinestone pin and a yellow linen dress. In Astoria the prints hung over my parents' twin beds. They were the only adornment in the room. 'Framed at Macy's,' she'd proudly say.

They bring me back to Astoria and how after Mammie died, Carey threw all her stuff out.

There was no point confronting him. Carey was dying for any excuse to clap me across the face. Out went her clothes. Out went her pocketbooks and the potato baker, blackened beyond use, but still able to produce a tasty potato. All that was left was a few bags of letters and photos. Going through them would take more time than Carey was willing to give, so I took them.

In the snaps my parents look happy. It's a summer afternoon in America somewhere in the country. Alice and Denis are in a field. A grand house looms in the background – a house where my mother must have worked as a maid. She's wearing a striped sun suit. He's in chinos.

There they are lying in a hammock.

There they are frolicking with the cows.

There they are wading in a stream.

There they are riding a tractor.

They're in love.

This was long ago. Long before Denis became 'Carey' and Mammie became 'Big Alice'. Long before Carey ran away from Kerry to become the playboy of the western world, but wound up a janitor at the Radio City Music Hall.

I see Alice frozen in black-and-white moments of happiness. I don't know her. This woman is not my

Mammie and I look away in embarrassment. She never told me about this part of her life.

There are a few snaps with me in them. There's Mammie and me in the back seat of a car. She's looking at Carey, who's taking the snap. She looks sad. They change places. Carey, a handsome wavy-haired big shot, sits next to me.

This is my family. These are the people with the hardened eyes of broken dreams that I remember. These are the people I lived with, in that freezing apartment in Astoria.

That we were tenants, not owners, cut Mammie to the quick. Renting a cold-water flat on the top floor of a terraced house proved Carey's failure for not being a better provider, and hers for having a soft heart and marrying him. Paying rent to a landlord, who neighbours say is a known fire fiend, salts her wound and questions Carey's sanity.

Still, the house is pretty with its two large elm trees out front, and the magnificent cherry out back. A few blocks away runs the East River. By the time it curves away from Manhattan to Queens its banks become rocky and rat infested.

'We're just across the river from Manhattan,' coos Mammie in her weekly letter *Home*.

Across the street is a Victorian mansion as scary as it is enticing. Mammie says it's an insane asylum. Sometimes we can hear inmates screaming at all hours.

With neither heat nor hot water we freeze in winter and roast in summer. Making dinner, we open every window in the place to accommodate grease from the frying pan.

Night after night, hat on her head, Mammie stands at the cooker, boiling water to wash the grease off the plates.

'Old mountaineer,' she jibes under her breath at Carey, who loves grease. Yet Astoria would have had to be better than living near the small village of Glenflesk, so far up 'the Paps' mountains, as they were called, you'd get a nosebleed from the climb.

* * *

It's Friday night. The radio's on. Carey's snoring on the couch. Mammie is pressing my school uniform skirt. I'm cutting Mitzi's beef liver into little bits and frying it in butter. All of us listening to the song John Wayne sipped his pint to in *The Quiet Man*.

I've met some folks who say that I'm a dreamer.
And I've no doubt there's truth in what they say.

Forty years onward I hear the same song in Bantry, booming out to the Square from O'Brien's Electric.

It's evening and I'm strolling around, looking at women coming from SuperValu, their trolleys full of jumbo-size this, jumbo-size that. I never have the need for jumbo anything.

O'Brien bumps up the sound. Bet he thinks it brings in customers. He'd never think of playing Van Morrison. Yet that song *meant* something to Carey and Mammie. The two of them there, locked in that kitchen with all that grease floating in the air, thinking thoughts of *Home*.

Down on the quay, the Whiddy Island ferry is pulling out. It's small, not like the large Fire Island ferries whizzing across the Great South Bay on a Friday night. Everyone greeted me on the ferry. Sometimes the bonhomie drove me crazy. Now I miss it.

A full moon is making its appearance over the Beara Peninsula. Over there beyond Caha, beyond Mangerton, beyond the Healy Pass is *Home*, Alice M'rie. The same moon will shine on the Fire Island ferries tonight. Christ! O'Brien's playing it again.

> *When the moonlight creeps across the rooftops*
> *I long to be back home in Innisfree.*

Which home am I in now?

7

A Priest & A Gala

Five a.m. and I'm wide awake, lying on my back on the floor of the stable. Silt settles on my face every time I change position, so I try and stay still. There's no breeze. I hear planes journeying up over Kerry and on to Shannon.

Geoffrey and I have been here for five days now, without electricity, phone or water. But yesterday the electrician popped by for a sec.

'I'm on my way to Hare Island,' he says, happy as a clam to be going over to Hare where, he says, there's great *craic*. He gets one socket going and the water pump. That's it. At least our first guest will be able to take a proper bath.

David LaGreca is the first friend I made after Scott's death. I met him on the train coming back from Fire Island, where I had just appeared in the Broadway musical *Damn Yankees*.

'You played that sports reporter like she was Diana Vreeland.'

I tell him I never talk to anyone on the train because I write. But somehow, we never shut up and a new friendship is born. Later that autumn at *Passion*, an unbearable new Stephen Sondheim musical, David reached over and touched my knee.

'This is worse than the Stations of the Cross.'

Thus was our friendship cemented, without my knowing David was once a priest. Now he's invited himself to Ireland to 'witness' as he put it, our first dinner party – The Gala, as I call it.

We could hardly miss him, standing smack in the apex of the village, all togged out in his new lemon-yellow I'll-face-the-rain-of-Ireland jacket. Instantly, the three of us let out a joyous whoop of recognition. A priest will bear witness to our chaos and he's even brought along *The New York Times*.

'Doll, this may be East Jesus, but you need to keep up.'

LaGreca did not bring a travelling crucifix in a leather box to place next to his bed like Father Bob did. Not that he has a bed to sleep in. He has the couch.

Threading through the rubble, cup of tea in hand, he says, 'Guys, do you know what they'd pay for these rocks on the Island?'

Then, in his commanding, priestly way, LaGreca spins into action by hooking up the washing machine.

'Just like being in the seminary in Belgium.'

Next, he washes down the fleet of painted chairs. 'Just like being in the Missions.'

And it's on to Dulux paint chips and colour testers.

'Dad was in the paint business.'

As I wash the floor for the umpteenth time, I watch LaGreca, all decked out in a red Lacoste polo shirt, washing windows. It's more than a little odd. The last time I was alone in a house with a priest was in Killarney with Father Bob, who wouldn't be caught dead in civvies. He always wore his Roman collar, except with his dressing gown.

A couple of bad memories fly around in my head. But I get rid of them by going out to a pile of rocks and taking deep breaths. Nothing bad can happen me here. Yet Father Bob, Sweet Afton dangling from the side of his mouth, walks right along with me.

'Well then, Alice M'rie, how 'bout a fag?'

'Ah no, Father Bob. It's bad for the complexion.'

'Grace Kelly smokes like a chimney.'

He and I would chat like that as we'd ride around Killarney in his black Morris Minor. The Paps of Anu, with cairns like two female breasts with nipples, come into view.

'Here we are then Alice M'rie, under the Paps. Sure you don't want a drag?'

Father Bob fades and LaGreca appears. Priests ... even now, I'm still afraid of them.

* * *

It's the night of the Gala. Who needs electricity with the sun still shining at ten? The glow from oil lamps and candles caresses the walls. A huge linen tablecloth covers floor planks on sawhorses that we'll use as a table.

The Aga is cooking a stuffed pork roast on one rack, while Fred Astaire's daughter Ava's potatoes, simmering with cream and pancetta, are on the other. A frying pan filled with Bramley apples and lemons bubbles away on the simmering plate. The white wine has been chilling all day in the well.

Musicals blast out to the fields – only happy ones. *Guys and Dolls* melts into *Kiss Me Kate* to blend into *Cabaret* and become *A Little Night Music*.

LaGreca dons a blazer, Geoffrey and I our all-purpose black. We stand outside holding wine glasses to wait for the first guests this building has ever had. Had I the recording, I'd play the Humming Chorus from *Madama Butterfly* to accompany the crickets chirping their autumn riff.

We stand in the rubble looking over the mountains towards Bantry Bay. Three New Yorkers bound by the friendship of another island, and by the scars of AIDS. Comfortable silence, holy silence, descends on us.

'It's a benediction,' says LaGreca.

Down on the road we hear cars whirr by on their way to where? Three are heading here.

Geoffrey and I have managed to make friends through the magic circle of 'six degrees of separation' – Ava being a prime example. She and her husband, portrait painter Richard McKenzie, have lived in west Cork for over twenty-five years. At Gay Men's Health Crisis, Geoffrey worked with Lars Jahns, who knew Ava and told us to call her. Now she and Richard have become our courage, Richard sealing our fate by saying, 'Yes, there *is* a special aura about west Cork.'

Ava and Richard had told us to call drama critic Gordon Rogoff and his partner, painter Morton Lichter. On the weekend we first saw this house we gave them a call. Our friendship began over mince tarts and mulled wine. In turn they introduced us to the Collins sisters,

Moira and Deirdre, standard-bearers of west Cork mores and style.

If this sounds like a comedy of manners with so-and-so knowing so-and-so that was married to the ex-wife of so-and-so, it's true. West Cork runs that way. Everyone here knows everyone's business.

Three cars arrive at once and as everyone hobbles over the rubble they all start squealing.

'You two … you really did it!'

'Better be careful, marriages break up redoing old houses.'

Over the past months, everyone had come by to check on progress. But the stable by candlelight is magic. The grey walls have taken on a medieval glow as everyone troops from room to room ooh-ing at the sunset reflected on jam jars full of daisies, purple loosestrife and Queen Anne's lace placed on every windowsill.

So thrilled am I that everyone loves what we've done, I launch into a spiel on painted *Irish* houses, as if everyone didn't know about them already. I rattle on about how vivid colour combats the grey of winter. That's why I want to paint every room here, and in the Big House, a different colour. But Deirdre interrupts to say that Jeremy Irons loves the grey walls of his castle by Roaringwater Bay, and won't paint them.

Soon everyone is sitting around on the painted chairs, drinking wine and callooing and callaying, leaving Richard and me to walk back and forth. 'Remarkable,' he mutters. 'Remarkable.'

In a building that's never heard a note of music, we introduce it to 1930s dance bands played on our new boom box. Cole Porter mixes with Noel Coward and everyone starts dancing.

'This is it! This is my dream!' I think, as Gordon and I face the music, and dance. Who needs electricity or a phone when, as Cole Porter wrote, a full 'August moon, burning above', shines outside the open Dutch door?

I'm dizzy with exhaustion, wine, dancing and triumph. For no reason at all, except that Alice M'rie once loved it, I start in quoting a favourite line from *Auntie Mame*, one of Miss D.'s hits.

'Oh, no more champagne, Lord Dudley. The bubbles no longer tickle my nose.' And I say it over and over again.

The dancing is fierce. Ava takes pictures of Moira and LaGreca out on the cobbles, Richard and Deirdre over by the well and Geoffrey and me in front of the Aga, shimmying like Romans in the Temple of Hera.

8

Skellig Michael

The day after the Gala we leave at the crack of dawn for a pilgrimage to Skellig Michael.

Near Waterville, where the road cuts near the coast, we see them: two foreboding jagged shapes, jutting out of the Atlantic Ocean. The Skelligs. I've known about them all my life. Mammie and Father Bob used them as place references. We'd be tooling around in his car, me on the map.

'Mammie, where's Valentia?'

'Oh, somewhere out by Skelligs.'

LaGreca is sitting in the back, cap on head, marvelling that we aren't listening to RTÉ, but playing show tunes. *Sweeney Todd* blasts out into the Caha Mountains. There isn't a lyric Geoffrey and I don't know and don't bellow out to the sheep below.

'This is like Fellini, you guys. *This* is like Fellini,' says LaGreca, complimenting us, I think, for blasting show tunes onto the sheep-covered mountain.

Our car swerves past hordes of sheep, their forelocks splashed in hot pink, blocking the road, putting us in danger of careening down the pass.

I'm beginning to feel uncomfortable with the priest in the back. Put it away, Alice M'rie. Throw all those old wounds out the window and watch them crash into the ocean.

We stop in Waterville for lunch at the Butler Arms, once Charlie Chaplin's hangout and immediately, Geoffrey's off to the phones trying to reach Johnnie K.

'So, listen,' asks LaGreca,' tell me about this Father Bob.'

'He was just a priest.'

'No one's *just* a priest.'

I say nothing.

'Was he a diocesan priest?'

'Well, he wasn't a Jesuit, that's for sure.' And we laugh, for LaGreca once was.

'But he was the sun, the moon and the stars to Mammie, myself as well. We were pen pals. Wrote all the time, grown-up stuff about movies, movie stars. He thought it funny I belonged to the James Mason fan club.'

'I think it's funny,' says LaGreca.

'His hair looked like Mason's – black, wavy, lots of it. Said he never washed it. That's why it wasn't grey.'

'Now you tell me,' says LaGreca rubbing his hand over his shaved pate.

'I'd write to him for Irish books and he'd send them off to Astoria. *A School History of Ireland*, in two volumes, Moore's *Melodies*. I still have them. Cards with black kittens with red bows wishing me good luck in my exams.

'Then one summer when Mammie brought me back, and I looked sort of grown-up you know, hair in a bun, blazer, penny loafers, I guess he got a crush on me.'

'That's not what we call it "inside",' says LaGreca.

* * *

That particular summer Mammie said, 'Bob's got a girlfriend.' Everyone loved it. After Sunday Mass at the Friary, he and I would stroll around town hand in hand, with Mammie bringing up the rear.

I liked him. He was funny, Englishy. He'd say things like 'cheerio', 'luv', 'brolly'. I had to get used to his calling cigarettes fags. He'd buy me loads of Cadbury bars and any book I wanted.

'Alice M'rie, the Irish milk from the Irish cows, that comprise the Irish Cadbury chocolate bar is far superior to milk from the English cows.' That's what Father Bob said as he stroked my hand.

Jesus, he was a stiff old Mass-sayer! He went by the book. *Doe-mee-nous-voh-bees-cummm*. Mammie and I'd laugh. No fast in-and-out at the Friary when Father Bob took centre stage.

The length of his Mass drove us crazy, and sometimes she and I would trot down to the Cathedral for a quickie – half-hour-on-the-nose-with-sermon! Yet even as we knelt with the 'townies', as Mammie called them, looming over our heads was the promise of a 'special indulgence' if we heard Father Bob's Mass, and received Holy Communion from his very own hand.

Mary and Dave truly believed if the Slattery family attended Father Bob's Mass the lot of us would get a special indulgence, so if we died together we'd fly right up to heaven.

Mammie and I knew this was superstition, but deep in our hearts we believed a teeny bit of it. (I even wondered how could we all die together.) So we'd make a few appearances at the Friary over the summer to partake.

We'd grit our teeth and hold our breath at the smell of Father Bob's nicotine-stained fingers as he put the wafer on our tongues.

After Mass, it was off to the Arbutus for dinner, an all-afternoon event. A huge table was reserved for Father Bob, ourselves and a few invited neighbours thrilled to bits to be sharing a meal with the Father.

Everyone at the Arbutus bent over backwards for him: starched tents of linen napkins and ashtrays stationed at every other seating; they even had Lucifers, those strong wooden matches in pocket-sized boxes featuring a drawing of a swallow.

Soldiers of Guinness lined up the centre. Coasters with little fawns gambolling among the stars proclaiming: *Oh I'd Love A Babycham* – the girl's drink. Steaming blue platters of well-cooked lamb and peas, two heavy gravy boats and three big bowls each holding a different kind of potato: mashed, boiled and chipped.

Father Bob stationed himself and me at the head of the table, sort of like bride and groom, his hand clasped over mine on his knee, shielded by the white linen tablecloth.

First he'd take a big draught of Guinness. Then he'd line up his peas on the tines of his fork and hold court.

'It's a terrible thing today, all the young girls killed in England. Drugs, you see, drugs and lads joyriding around.

Just the other night I was called to an accident by the roundabout at Sainsbury's. Terrible. Terrible. Raining. Bank holiday as well. The lad was dead. T.G. he wasn't Catholic.'

'Now Bob, how do ye know that?' chirps Mammie, hanging on his every word.

'The girl told me. Poor thing. Died in my arms … her jugular severed.'

That silenced the table and Dave bleats, 'Whist, Alice M'rie, pass the lamb.'

Father Bob releases my hand, and I push the lamb over to Dave. Not missing a beat, he continues.

'I bent down to give her absolution. The poor girl, a lovely redhead, can barely speak. '"Father, Father, bless me Father for I have sinned", the usual stuff. The blood was everywhere. Joan, my housekeeper, said it took a whole box of carbolic to clean my collar. The girl was fading. "My daughter …" I call them daughter for the transference. Alice M'rie knows all about that.'

'I do?'

'Father, daughter.'

'No, I don't.'

Father Bob squeezes my hand again against his fat knee.

'"Tell me your confession," I say to the poor girl.'

'"O Father, impure …"'

'She died in my arms. Fast cars. Fast women. Oh Alice M'rie, the sixties are a terrible time to be young in.'

''Tis true, Father Bob, 'tis true,' says an old hen breathing in his every utterance as she passes around a tin of snuff.

Another platter of lamb arrives and before it hits the table, Father Bob whispers into my ear, 'Alice M'rie, do you pray to the patron saint of Youth Purity, Saint Maria Goretti?'

'All us girls do. I've a picture of her. She's pretty.'

'Whist, Alice M'rie,' croaks Dave. 'Stop hoggin' the spuds.' Father Bob releases my hand and I pass the spuds.

* * *

The Butler Arms waitress is hovering. Any talk at all of priests and they loiter. Paedophilia is on everyone's brain.

'And the special today is roast lamb.'

LaGreca peers over his glasses.

'With potatoes?'

'Yes, sir, we have three kinds – chips, boiled and mashed.'

'I'll have all three.'

* * *

We book a B&B on Valentia Island for the night. The next morning dawns fair and as we approach the quay at Portmagee, Charons and their boats await us. All big, all strong, but it's Peter Mackey who stands apart.

'I hope he's our boatman,' says LaGreca. And you'd have to be blind not to think that yourself. Peter Mackey is the Man of Aran and the Flying Dutchman rolled up together in a raggy woollen sweater. There isn't a finer boatman to be had in all of Ireland.

'He looks like Gabriel Byrne,' says LaGreca, as Peter lends him a shaky hand to board the vessel.

'I'm nursing off th'night,' says Peter, giving him a wink.

Peter's boat holds about thirty people, all of them eager to be tortured, all talking out loud to ease their fear of *Fear* by saying the same things.

'Ooooh, look at the headlands.'

'*Boy!* They're green all right!'

'Next parish America.'

Everyone's read the guidebooks, so everyone knows that Skellig Michael is neither for the weak nor the faint-hearted. Once we get there, if we do, we're stuck till Peter returns to rescue us.

The first half hour is an easy-peasy, cruising-down-the-river-on-a-Sunday-afternoon sort of thing. Then we leave the headlands and enter the Atlantic. This is not a mere boat ride. Considering Fire Island, where the sea is a killer, you'd think I'd have inkling. I haven't a clue.

In our breezy New York way we've come prepared with sunblock, caps, chocolate bars, grapes and water. Yet we're not prepared for the sight of a barren 715-foot-high rock mountain charging straight up from the sea, daring the lot of us to climb to its summit.

From curve of shore to bend of bay, Peter's boat rises and dips with the currents. Bosch's painting of the Ship of Fools flashes in my head. That is what we look like – all of us hanging on for dear life – one hand on the railing, one on a camera.

'We may get lucky an' get dolphins on the way back,' says Peter, fag drooping from his mouth. 'That's 'cause there're no gales or swells today. If we had 'em, I'd be back in the pub and yuz all ud be disappointed.'

As hundreds of gannets soar above, eyeballs lock in terror. Fearsome currents have us sliding like a deck of cards. Peter eases the boat near Little Skellig, so we can take pictures of this mountain white from gannet guano, which, LaGreca says, the monks dried and used for currency and fuel.

Hundreds of birds swirl above in a vortex of disruption. Some dive-bomb the boat. Cool ones remain on the rocks. They've seen it all. As far back as the

Middle Ages pilgrims made this trek. And for what, to get a blessing from St Michael like Mammie and I thought we'd get from Father Bob?

Soon we dock at a stone pier covered in sea-grass slime. Peter helps us off, LaGreca thrilled to be offered a sinewy arm to grasp onto. Now we're on our own. No restrooms, snack bars or telephones, though there is a helicopter pad, in case a pilgrim gets smited.

After an easy walk on cement steps with people cheering, 'This is nothing. You should try Croagh Patrick,' there looms in front of us the thousand-year-old stone stairway of 600 steps. Now I understand why the monks who came here in the sixth century thought this island to be the end of the world itself.

Geoffrey leads the way. LaGreca brings up the rear with me in the middle, like the cream in an Oreo cookie. It's hot. Barren. Grecian. This isn't Ireland. This is a place beyond. One minute I'm scorched by sun. The next minute the hairs on my arms are standing up from the cold wind. The air is needle sharp. It's scary. There are no guardrails, fences or barricades to prevent me from hurling myself into the dark Atlantic.

I think of Carey. How at his most venomous he'd give us a surprise call from JFK to announce, 'I'm going to

Ireland and jump off the Cliffs of Moher.' Mammie and I always hoped he would.

We climb up a level, take a rest. Up another, take a picture, up another, a swig of water, a daub of sun block. Sweat drips from us. People are dropping like flies and returning to the concrete platform, which at this point seems comfy.

The higher up we get, the steeper the steps. So steep I can no longer walk upright, and have to climb up on my hands and knees.

The higher up I get, the further I am from the world as I know it. I become obsessed with the sun, the unrelenting sun permeating the straw brim of my hat and burning my nose. I peer down, down to the cool, dark blue velvet of the Atlantic with not a Lorelei to greet me if I jump.

In a delirium that only unrelenting sun can induce, I wonder if I did jump would I not become part of the Celtic Twilight? Would I not join in spiritual communion with the monks?

Near the summit there's a psychedelic-green glade called the Saddle, covered with thickly matted watercress-like vegetation the monks used for food. It's our first chance to sit and, in unison, we pilgrims take a break. Suspended in this green glen in the sky, everyone picnics, peeling bananas, slugging water and scarfing down Kit-Kats.

It's so psychedelic, so trippy that I start singing, 'Lucy in the sky with diamonds,' as we peer up to the summit for a glimpse of the six beehive-shaped stone huts where the monks lived, worked, and died.

Literally and figuratively, LaGreca is in heaven.

'This is fabulous! Those monks were cra-zee!'

They'd have to be. I imagine monks without morning tea, chanting into the pre-light of dawn to God. Monks in their woolly robes, sweating bullets, deranged from eating cress, and the occasional roast seagull or puffin. Monks, with nary a drop of the *craythur* to soothe their souls if they got blue.

Maybe they kept bees? Maybe they made mead? Did the monks not want to get drunk like pagans would, to worship their God?

Would they not worship the sun? Surely the sun rules Skellig Michael, not God, as we know him? The monks must have believed this. How could they not? Did they not build their beehive dwellings facing west to the setting sun, to the land of *Tir na nÓg*?

I get a faraway look in my eye.

'Alice Marie, are you okay?' asks LaGreca.

'I'm not Alice M'rie no more.'

'Sweet Saint Joseph, the nearer she gets to heaven, the more she forgets her grammar.'

'Sorry, the sun's addled my brain.'

We proceed to the summit. Had I had the strength to run, I would to escape the sun for the stony cool of a beehive hut. We're so far up in the sky, I feel strangely one with the Mother Mary blue sky and not a cloud in sight.

I wander off from the men to a dangerous edge. Way away over there, veiled in mist, is Ireland. I can barely make it out. Ireland where I came from, and Mammie came from and Carey came from. Ireland where people pray for sun, never wear sunblock and burn to a crisp when they visit the Mediterranean – Ireland that's me and I it.

After taking a potential Christmas card photo, and a few shrieks of *Faaaaabulous* from LaGreca, the three of us start looking down to see if Peter Mackey has come to our rescue.

There is a frisson of excitement in the air. Everyone feels it. We have achieved our goal. We got to the Skelligs and we climbed to the top. Yet I feel strangely sad. If I had my druthers I'd rather be back in New York.

Alice M'rie, admit it, you miss your Mammie. You miss someone you don't even remember. You miss your Mammie, whose voice you've all but forgotten.

It occurs to me that this summit was the place Mammie pointed to from the *Mauretania* oh so many years ago, when I was young and she was not yet old. Again, LaGreca catches the faraway look in my eye. It takes a priest.

'Doll ... tell me.'

'Oh, I'm looking at Ireland over there and thinking what it was like coming back to Kerry of a summer with my mother. We could see the Skelligs from the ship. On board everything seemed so full of promise. We had such high hopes then.'

9

Mauretania

On the *Mauretania* dawn arrived around 4.30 in the morning. And on the day we were scheduled to dock in Cobh, Mammie and I crept out of bed at four, put on our arrival outfits, and scampered upstairs to Main Deck to see the dawn on the hills of Ireland.

'Mammie … it's a fine day.'

And it is. A dreamy, grey-apple-green day, made sweeter with the knowledge that it could just as easily be a dark, dank, rainy one. In the chilly dawn, stewards are walking around with trays of steaming cups of tea, pre-mixed with milk and sugar. In the distance is the rocky Kerry coast. I can barely make it out.

'Mammie, do you know where we are?'

'By the Skelligs. See there. See the top of that rock.'

She gets silent. She's looking way beyond the horizon, way, way over there, beyond the Skelligs, beyond Mangerton Mountain, beyond the Lakes of Killarney.

'Mammie, what're you looking at?'

'I'm looking Home, *Home*, Alice M'rie. Dave and Father Bob are just getting into the cars to meet us.'

As the *Mauretania* inches nearer the coast, we start picking out the outlines of stone cottages. First one, then another, then another would light up; and men going out to the haggard to milk the cows, women putting the kettle on for tea.

All over Ireland tea is being poured into cups, just like it is on deck. At that moment everyone on land and on sea is united by this lovely drink. This balm that warms the hands as it warms the heart, this cup of tea.

Silence. Oh, the silence of the passengers. All of them, rich and poor, tourist and diaspora, clutching cups in the early morning damp, hoping, all of them, hoping this summer there'll be less drink. Hoping this summer will be nice. Hoping this summer will be warm. Hoping this summer will be less damp. Hoping. Hoping. I see it in their faces. Me too. I'm hoping the Slatterys will be glad, and I'll be glad, and Mammie'll be glad we've come *Home*.

Alice's mother, Alice Slattery, in front of her family home in Carrigeen, County Kerry, in the 1920s.

Alice, aged seven, on her way to Mass with her Mammie in 1950s Astoria, New York.

Ten-year-old Alice attempts to look sophisticated in a 'grown-up' white dress.

Alice, aged twelve, atop a steamer trunk, all set to board the *Mauretania* the next day on her first trip 'home' to Ireland.

Alice in Astoria, New York, in the 1950s.

Above: Alice with the Slattery dogs in Carrigeen's haggard in County Kerry, early 1960s.

Right: Fifteen-year-old Alice about to make her first plane ride home, trying to look like Princess Grace.

JUN • 66

Alice's parents, Denis and Alice Carey, in Killarney, 1966. This is the only photo Alice has of her parents in Ireland.

Above: Father Bob with his beloved Morris car, Carrigeen, County Kerry, 1960s.

Left: Fifteen-year-old Alice with her uncle Father Bob, in front of the Slattery house in County Kerry.

Trailblazing Broadway producer Jean Dalrymple (Miss D. to Alice) and her husband, Major General Philip de Witt Ginder, at a ball in the Waldorf Astoria in the 1950s.

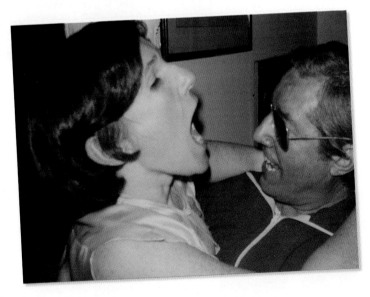

Alice dancing with Homer Poupart, one of Miss D.'s office boys, at a Halloween party she and Geoffrey threw in their Greenwich Village apartment in 1974.

Alice and Geoffrey on Fire Island, New York, in winter, 1980s.

Alice and Geoffrey at an AIDS
march in Washington DC, 1992.

Geoffrey and Alice in front of their beloved
beach house, the 'Magic Flute', on Fire
Island, New York, in 1988.

This is Alice and Geoffrey's first glimpse, and first picture, of the derelict stable in west Cork they fell in love with in November 1994.

The restored stable in 2000: a dream come true. Enormous patience, a bright red door and blue hydrangeas complete the picture.

First glimpse of the Big House, November 1994. When Alice and Geoffrey showed the photo to their New York friends, they thought them crazy.

The Big House in spring 2014, turned gloriously orange over time. It is painted with copperas provided by neighbour Jeremy Irons, who used it on his nearby castle.

Above: Geoffrey walks up the lane to the Big House with Thomasina the cat during a bleak west Cork winter in 2013.

Left: Geoffrey and Alice play 'Adam and Eve' in their apple orchard in 2010.

Tea finished, the stewards start passing out whiskey. Even to me. A nip in the hand to take off the chill and warm the soul, to give courage where prayer fails. Then the singing begins. A man with a squeeze-box begins singing come-all-ye's.

I'll take you home again Kathleen.
Across the ocean wild and wide.

Sobbing begins.

To where your heart has ever been
Since first you were my bonny bride.

Mammie stifles back a cry, her tears hidden by her veil.

A gong sounds. Breakfast is announced. The sun pops out. The crying stops. Quick as a flash, everyone bursts into loud cries of 'Thank God it's a fine day.' Then we all sit down to a big breakfast, putting the lining in our bellies for the long day ahead.

Announcements are made to board the tender.

Bang! The class system ends.

Cheek by jowl, passengers from all three classes jostle together: all of us, going home to Ireland.

As we approach St Colman's Cathedral I get scared. Being here for six weeks might not be easy. It might deflate the starch in my dresses and the pizzazz in Mammie's hats.

She's going back to her family. To the Slatterys who knew her when she was a girl. To the Slatterys who remember her hopes and know her secrets. To people who hope she'll be the way she was when she left. And she's bringing me, the fruit of her womb. She's bringing me. Me, with my *Hello, dar-ling*! Alice M'rie, drop those airs. You're going to Carrigeen, a wide spot on the road to Killarney.

Mammie is gazing over to St Colman's. Do I dare take her picture? Yes, I should. It's a glamorous church. It must have beautiful weddings. I'll take a picture of Mammie looking at St Colman's.

'Mammie ...'

She doesn't answer. She seems different. Yet she looks the same. There's her oatmeal dress. There's her white straw hat and veil. There's her gloves. Yet my Mammie's going through a metamorphosis. She's becoming Irish again. *Irish*, I tell you. Irish like Kathleen Ní Houlihan, Maud Gonne, Queen Meabh and that I'll-take-you-home-again-Kathleen-girl, all rolled into one. Did this change start when she took off her gloves?

Maybe it started when she lifted the veil off her face for a minute to get a better view of St Colman's? Maybe it started when the man with the squeeze-box began playing war songs.

We'll meet again, don't know where don't know when,
But I know we'll meet again some sunny day.

First Class and Third Class are singing together. Mammie too, singing along heartily.

As the tender approaches the dock we see people madly waving at us. Everyone looks so dour – tweeds, caps, jackets, dark, dark, dark. Mammie and I look like two trimmed Christmas trees.

The man starts in again with come-all-ye's. And all the Irish start to cry again. I feel a part of it all, yet a stranger to it all. My head is spinning. I don't know who I am.

I'm Alice M'rie. I'm Little Alice. I'm Alice Carey. Who do I want to be here?

Mammie spots her brother David and she starts waving madly.

'Dave! Dave! We're here! We're here!'

My Mammie's completely Irish now. And me? I'm … Irish American. No, I'm not. I'm not at all like the Irish Americans around me wearing green to prove that they are. Everyone set to kiss the Blarney Stone. I'm an Irish New Yorker. That's who I am.

Alice M'rie, leave your airs on the tender. For the next six weeks you'll be Irish, just like your Mammie. That's what you want to be – the real article. Right?

* * *

Standing on the dock in a straight line are the Slatterys. Father Bob in clerical black, his long, shiny, patent leather hair severely parted in the middle, like Charlie Chaplin's. Next to him, his older brother, grizzled old Dave in his battered tweed cap. A little apart, hands clasped behind his back, my cousin D.D., heir to the farm, in his rugby blazer with gold crest. The lot smoking Sweet Aftons through nicotine-stained fingers.

Father Bob whisks us through Customs, in that cool and breezy way priests have, and indeed the Red Sea parts. The inspectors knowing they'll be nearer to God for the favour.

Two black Morris Minors await our trunks, a Victrola, records and scads of presents. We're laden down with summer shirts for Dave, striped ties for D.D. and his brother, Robert; and 'full figure' blouses for Dave's wife, Mary Falvey. Mammie gets in the car with Dave and D.D. I'm left with Father Bob.

'Well then, Alice M'rie … how 'bout a fag?' Father Bob lights up an Afton and lets it fall to the side of his mouth.

'Ah, no Father Bob. Ladies don't smoke.'

We carry on. Banter, you know. What I'm good at. Being pen pals, we don't have much to fill in. I don't tell him that in Miss D.'s office *fag* is a loaded word. I do tell him I'm in love with James Mason.

Dave and the lads announce they're 'dyin' of thirst', so we stop in Cork city for a drink and a bite at the Metropole.

'Ah, Father,' coos the barmaid. 'Ye're back for the summer again. May it be a fine one, please God.' Stationing herself nearer to me she goes on. 'And is this the girl? Isn't she nice and big!'

I settle into my Orange Squash, knowing this too will pass. Women like her talk that way. They never shut up.

'Is she going to be a nun?'

Be polite, Alice. She's only a barmaid sucking up to a priest. Doesn't she see I'll be a star? She'd know if she'd seen me do my imitation of Julie Andrews. Aw, she wouldn't know Julie if she fell on her.

'No, Eily,' I say icily, reading her name tag, 'I don't think God's calling me.'

'Not yet anyway,' says Father Bob, pulling my ponytail and tucking into his pint.

* * *

The road from Cork to Kerry is long and flat. I'm sleepy and Father Bob's woozy from Guinness. He switches on a radio call-in show.

'And now, a very special birthday greeting for a Mrs Bridie Joyce way up there in Malin Head, from her son stationed down in Portarlington. "Cutting the Corn in Creeslough Today", sung by the lovely Ruby Murray. It's a grand day to be cutting the corn, or the turf, or corners, for all you working girls out there. Take it away, Ruby.' After a summer of this, I'll be crying for Tony Bennett.

I dangle my arm outside the window and let the breeze run through my fingers. The Kerry Mountains are in the distance. The cows are standing up. Father Bob says that means it'll be a fine day.

He's already proclaimed the heat's killin' him. Of course, he hasn't taken off his wool jacket. Up ahead I see our steamer trunk strapped onto Dave's car. I can hear Mammie laugh. Father Bob hears her too, and he pats my knee.

'Alice M'rie, isn't it nice yourself and Alice have come home.'

'O yes, it's great to be here.'

Liar!

Carrigeen is not my home. My home is Manhattan. My home is on the East Side where there are lovely private houses with blue morning glories twined around the railings. My home is the Lexington Avenue coffee shop where I languish over a chocolate malted and tuna sandwich. (Extra mayo, please.) My home is sitting on the floor in Miss D.'s office, talking to Homer. My home isn't Astoria or Carrigeen. My home is all the places I hope will be my home someday.

* * *

The Paps come into view, then the fields and then the house. In the doorway stands Mary Falvey, fly swatter in her hefty hand.

I take a gander at her. She's a big woman with one eye looking straight up to Heaven, the good one staring straight out in an unblinking gaze. Mary Falvey does not drive. This must be the reason why.

Behind Mary Falvey's head dangles a twirl of flypaper covered with dead blue bottles. One of the first things Mammie does when we go into Killarney is to buy several rolls of fresh flypaper.

'So here's the girl then. O' Alish M'rie, aren't ye fine and big?'

Fine? Big? What is this woman insinuating?

Fine? It must be my blazer, with its lovely crest signifying nothing. *Big*? She must mean, tall. But I'm short. It's a terrible thing to be short. On stage I'll be tall. Just like Julie Andrews. Homer says Julie makes all sorts of people believe she's really tall, by thinking tall. Does Mary Falvey mean *fat* then? Not me. Not fat. Never. I'll swear off sweeties. I'll never darken a bakery's door again.

My cousin Robert ambles out. He's wearing a blazer, but without a crest. He's got a few grey hairs. Mammie too. And Carey. Maybe it runs in the family. I'll never be grey. I'll listen to Father Bob.

'That's the secret, Alice M'rie; never wash your hair. Just grease it up. Preserves the colour. I use Royal Crown, just like Prince Philip.'

We enter the house, go straight into the kitchen and for a good twenty minutes, we stand there on the cement floor with our coats on.

Father Bob asks Mary Falvey had she read the bog man story in the *Independent* about an old guy who'd just been found perfectly preserved in a bog up north, yellow buttercups in his mouth. She hadn't.

'Mind yourself, Alice M'rie, or the Bog Man'll get ye.' And Father Bob takes a big a swig of Paddy.

'Best whiskey in Ireland. Paddy is the daddy of them all.'

Mammie says, 'O Dave, say it again.' And he does.

Over in the corner near the fire I'm tucking into a large cup of the nicest, strongest, sweetest tea in the world and a Cadbury Dairy Milk bar.

There's so much to say, yet nothing to say. Mammie and Mary Falvey review the roll call of who's recently died. D.D. and Robert sit silently looking at the table. Father Bob and Dave are deep into a silent smoking session. I'm not sure they like each other, Father Bob being a big-shot priest and Dave being 'just' a farmer. Smoke covers up the awkwardness between them.

My eyes hit upon a large portrait of the Sacred Heart prominently displayed over the kitchen table, with Jesus' hand pointing to his heart. Big mistake back there at the Metropole. Jesus is not calling me, no matter what Eily the barmaid thinks.

Yet didn't 'poor' Mollie, who lived in a cloister in Sherwood Forest, wear her knees out praying I'd be a nun? If she prayed so much why did she get leukaemia? That's what I want to know.

I'm tired. Mammie's tired. It's damp. Our bellies are stuck to our backs with hunger. We want to settle in before the evening meal. We wait till Mary Falvey starts cleaning a kilo of newly dug-up spuds that are sitting in a basin of bog water. Then we go upstairs.

We've been put in Mary and Dave's room. I unpack my talismans and line them up on the night table. My framed picture of Mitzi, my diary, my pen and a small bottle of Diorissimo that Homer gave me. I lean my records against the wall next to my Victrola. *Carousel* must have broken on the ship.

Mammie has nothing on her side but reading glasses, an envelope of crime stories from the *Daily News* and a few pocket packs of Kleenex. She doesn't have a picture of Carey.

Mammie and I don't know the word *casual*. We don't have a casual bone in our bodies. You'd think we'd loosen up a bit on a farm – a pair of slacks for her, maybe jeans for me. 'But,' Mammie says, 'ladies don't wear trousers, not even Miss D.'

Mammie changes from her oatmeal-coloured dress to a black skirt and grey square-necked merino sweater with pearls. Pearls! Can you beat it? Pearls in the country with cows outside the window! But she does take off her hat. I take off my best pink cotton dress with two crinolines and put on a plaid skirt and navy sweater. I'm freezing. We both are.

We haven't had a chance to pee since the Metropole. Mammie checks under the bed for the 'po'. Out comes the Kleenex and down we squat. Terrible. I've just begun to get my period. But we don't talk about that. I've three boxes of Modess in my suitcase and a white cotton panty, with rubber crotch liner, to prevent a thin red line appearing on a white dress.

'*Modess … because*' hiss the glamorous magazine adverts with all those beautiful women standing around in satin evening gowns. The lot of them happy to be bleeding into '*Modess … because*'. I don't know if Mammie's still bleeding. She could be. She looks young enough, then again maybe not. We don't share grown-up stuff like that.

Mammie says she'll have to burn my napkins when the men are out. Do all mothers burn their daughters' menstrual blood?

That done we wash our faces in a basin filled with freezing bog water that looks brown. That's the way it is. Mammie says so … and it's good for the complexion. Then, as the smell of boiled potatoes mixed with Sweet Afton wafts up the stairs, Mammie and I go down to dinner.

10

On the Farm

Each day is like the other. No matter what the day, occasion, or holiday, Slattery cows are milked by hand by 5 a.m. Then the milk is driven by horse cart to the creamery.

Dawn is breaking over the Paps. Mammie and I are woken in our bed with this.

'D.D. get up ... get up, I say ... D.D.'

This is 'The Ballad of Mary Falvey', and it sounds like this:

> *Dayyyyyy-deeee!*
> *Git up.*
> *Git up oi-shayyyyyy.*

Mary Falvey never varies her lines. And D.D. never gets up till the ballad is repeated many times. Once in a while Dave chirps in with a 'Whist, Day Dee ... listen to eer Mother.' But D.D. remains asleep, only to wake when Mary Falvey gets to her feet, marches into his room and rattles the bed frame.

I try to go back to sleep, but I'm smothered under the weight of a quilt so heavily stuffed with cotton batten, and cross-hatched with stitches and buttons, it's impossible to turn over. Next door, we hear Father Bob snoring away. Nothing wakes him.

After a day or two, Father Bob starts coming into our room in the morning without knocking, but Mammie and I don't mind at all. We're so relieved not to see Carey's face. After all, he is a priest. Priests do what they like.

What he's doing is holding out the promise of London. But before London, we'll have to go to Liverpool and visit Bootle, where he's just been appointed pastor of a brand-new church in a brand-new parish. Mammie's thrilled to bits the Slatterys will have a P.P. in the family. But 'liverpool' sounds pretty grim to me.

'O Bob, your first church. Alice M'rie's so excited to see it.'

I'm not. I want to go to London.

'Now Bob, tell me. Ye're at Our Lady of ... where?'

'Walsingham.'

'Isn't that where the Royal family stays?'

'That's Windsor, Alice.'

So we put up with his early-morning appearances. The door opens and there's the new P.P. of Our Lady of some place I've never heard of, large and resplendent in his green damask bathrobe, with black tassels.

'Well then Alice, it's a fine day to be up and about. Alice M'rie, no dreaming of James Mason, now.'

Mammie and I don't respond to such chatter and pretend to be sleeping. We breathe a sigh of relief when Father Bob leaves and bounds downstairs all fired up to consume a breakfast of three fried eggs, four rashers, four sausages, a healthy slice of black pudding, several slices of brown bread slathered with butter and marmalade and an entire pot of tea so strong you can stand up a spoon in it.

Since Mammie can't drive we're dependent on Father Bob to take us into Killarney, or 'town' as she calls it. A bus passes the door at 11.30 a.m, and returns at 3.30 p.m., but Mammie thinks using public transportation to visit her own town is beneath her station. So we pray for Father Bob to suggest a trip, which insures our making a day, and sometimes a night, of it.

Killarney *is* Ireland to me. It's the only town I know. Everyone talks about Dublin like it's a distant metropolis, with cinemas, department stores and restaurants. Killarney has none of these, and it's not really pretty. But it is a town. It's all I have. And I live to go there.

Father Bob's all chuffed because he finally passed his driver's test in Liverpool. He's thrilled with his new Morris, and he never shuts up about how England's roads are better than Ireland's, because after the War they were all rebuilt.

Even so, Father Bib drives really slowly. Going to town with D.D takes twenty minutes. It takes a half hour with him. I tell you, if a lorry took a lunge at us, we'd be dead on the road from his poor reflexes.

Putt … putt … putt … goes the Morris.

'A lorry, Bob,' screams Mammie. 'A lorry!' *Screeeeeech*.

Father Bob jams the brakes and the Morris stalls. Hand upon the gearstick he chants the same old litany every time this happens: 'Oh dear … Oh my … Oh goodness … Oh gracious … Oh mercy me.'

If really challenged he'll let out with a 'Jesus, Mary and Saint Joseph!'

You'd think a man of his P.P. stature would say, 'Oh shite, oh piss, oh feck,' and be done with it, but no. Worse, his incompetence is aided by Mammie's unflagging support.

'Oh, I love driving with Bob. He goes so lovely and slow.' This is the man who's going to show me London!

When we get to Killarney, Father Bob makes a beeline to the Arbutus for a pint, leaving Mammie and me to amble around the streets.

As New Yorkers, we're used to change. So we half expect Killarney to change as well. But just as 'The Ballad of Mary Falvey' never changes, neither does Killarney. The same pink-and-yellow gateaux, striped bullseyes and hard-boiled sweets in the sweet shop windows that look like they've hung around for years. Cans of Batchelors Mushy Peas have faded from green to grey, and the Jaffa oranges are rusted.

Our first stop is the butcher. Mammie and I love our butchers. Sometimes seeing a just-killed chicken eviscerated right before my eyes is the high point of my day.

'Ah Missus, this chicken was sayin' his prayers this very mornin'.'

'O Pat, have ye some lovely chops for us today?' Pat's chops have never been referred to as 'lovely' before, or since.

Onto a paper shop called the Favourite where they're saving the *London Sunday Times* for me.

'The girl's mad for reading.'

We weave through the lanes. Hello, cobbler. Hello, baker. Outside of an old hotel, The Imperial, Mammie tells of a distant cousin, a Miss Marie Slattery who owned it ages ago and cheated Mammie out of her rightful inheritance. The way Mammie's voice escalates, Miss Marie seems as real to her as yesterday. So we never go in.

It's hard navigating cobbled streets in my patent leather shoes with thrup'ny-bit heels, as Dave calls them. So when Mammie and I need a sit-down, depending on which side of town we wind up in, we go to the Friary or the Cathedral.

Mammie thinks the Friary is unfashionable. She doesn't say why. So we spend little time there. She loves the Cathedral where the 'townies' go to Mass. A Mass they come late to and leave early from – in before Gospel, out after Eucharist. And would you believe it, when I asked Father Bob about this, he said it isn't a sin!

We walk around this gigantic Gothic pile, admiring the life-sized Stations of the Cross, pretending we're having a good time. But we're not. What we're really doing is killing time. Mammie must be as bored with the slow pace of Killarney as I am.

After an Ave for *poor* Mollie's soul, and Father Bob's intentions – whatever they are – we head over to Muckross to visit the Sullivans, distant cousins who have a real bathroom.

* * *

At the Sullivans' I find my first boyfriend. Nothing serious, mind, 'cause he's religious. He's taken the Pledge and proudly wears that bleeding-heart pin on his lapel.

Haulie drinks ginger ale, doesn't smoke, doesn't dance and doesn't know who Julie Andrews is. But it was Haulie who paid attention to me.

Now believe you me, Haulie was no James Mason. But he paid me a compliment that made me smile. 'Twas he who gladdened my heart as we walked through the fairground that night after the bazaar.

It's a lingering July twilight. We're on our way back to the cars, Mammie, Father Bob, the Sullivans and me. Haulie and I are lagging behind, listening to the crickets.

'O Alice M'rie, dat's dem all right, rubbin' their legs together.'

We laugh. And as the sun's long fingers guide our way, words from an old poem pop into my head and I recite them to Haulie:

I was a child and he was a child
In that kingdom by the sea
And we loved with a love that was more than a love
I and my Annabel Lee.

'Go on then, Alice M'rie. Say it again.'

And I do. He thinks I wrote it. Haulie thinks I wrote *Annabel Lee,* and I let him think it.

'Ah Alice M'rie, ye're th'real article. That's what ye are, th'real article.'

That's what Haulie said. I loved it. And I loved him for saying it. I didn't mind that he was no James Mason, and for a few minutes we held hands. But Father Bob saw us, and next day he wanted to hold hands, too.

* * *

Days and nights flow together, beginning with 'The Ballad of Mary Falvey' and ending in a haze of Sweet Afton. No date has been chosen to go to London and Mammie doesn't seem to care. Though she's dying to see Father Bob's new church, I know she can live without seeing Harrods. She's just as happy sitting at the kitchen table, tracing relatives with Mary Falvey and drinking endless cups of tea.

'Oh yes, the Nagles of Blackwater … they're why *poor* Mollie became a nun.'

'Is that a fact?' says Mary.

'Ah Alice M'rie, ye'd have loved her.'

I don't ask why I would. I think 'it's raining, no going into Killarney today.'

'Why did Aunt Mollie become a nun?'

'Because of Nano Nagle. Alice M'rie, didn't I tell ye? You're related to a saint.'

Father Bob strolls in. 'I say, Alice, Nano isn't a saint yet. She's up for Beatification.'

Now with any talk of saints, my ears perk up. Oh, the gory mess of it all. I love it. Lady-saints like St Barbara, who got her breasts lopped off. *Whack*! Or St Catherine, strapped to that fiery wheel and twirled around and around till she dropped down dead. *Plop*!

None of that happened to Nano. All she did was found an order of nuns called the Irish Presentation Sisters. If it were up to me, only those who suffered horrible, terrible deaths would be saints. Founding an order of lady nuns doesn't cut the mustard.

Nickel to a doughnut, I bet Mammie and Father Bob are dying to see me dance down the road hand and hand with Nano and Mollie, and become a nun as well.

After a lull she starts rattling off the Slattery nuns.

'There's Eily and Kate in Texas. And Mother Mary Columcille in Cape Town.'

'And on the male side, Alice, let's not forget who says Mass. Yours truly … and Dan Joe.'

'But Bob, Dan Joe left the priesthood.'

'Ah yes, Alice, but once a priest always a priest. And our own little Alice M'rie one day … eh?' And he rubs the back of my neck.

Wink. Wink. Laugh. Laugh. *Bang*! goes the kettle. Out come a fresh pack of Aftons and a fresh pack of fig rolls. The constant rain is driving me nuts. Oh, the conspiracy of the three of them. Look at them wearing out the oilcloth with their elbows. Look at Father Bob all collared up, waiting to show off with something like an Extreme Unction. Look at Mammie in her hat, telling Mary Falvey she wears hats in the house because of the damp.

Oh no, Mary Falvey has gotten out a bag of snapshots, and they're eating them up.

Mammie (all teary): 'It's a grand thing our Mollie …'

Father Bob (lighting a fag): 'All these fine women sacrificing their lives.'

Mammie (looking at a picture of Mollie): 'Do ye remember how pretty she was?'

Father Bob (blowing a smoke ring): 'No.'

Mammie (prodding her finger in my back, reminding me I slouch): 'The Astoria nuns tell Alice M'rie ...'

Father Bob (grabbing my hand): 'That God is ...'

Mammie (prodding again): 'Calling her.'

Father Bob (letting my hand go): 'Alice M'rie, you didn't write me that. Tell us now.'

'Mammie, they haven't.'

* * *

The constant smoke from Sweet Afton drives me out to the haggard. There's no place to go. There's nothing to see, just a few smelly cows and an old pig wallowing in the hay. I could go upstairs and play *South Pacific*. That always cheers me up. But Mary Martin and her 'Cockeyed Optimist' crap won't work today.

Bet Mammie and Father Bob's plan is to drag me into *poor* Mollie's convent in Sherwood Forest and leave me there. I can see me standing, looking at *poor* Molly's grave, and those nuns grabbing me and slapping a white veil on my head.

Father Bob ambles out.

'Alice M'rie, I'm sorry. I fear we said the wrong thing, your mother and I. We were just joking. But you know, having a daughter a nun is a great assurance for a mother.'

''Tis.'

'Now then, Alice tells me this chap Homer has a special relationship with you.'

'Homer! Why would she mention Homer?'

'Do you hold hands?'

'No! He's a fairy! Didn't she tell you that as well?'

II

Oh, To Be In England

A few days later, Father Bob sets the date. We're on our way to London. His plan is to drive up to Dublin on Wednesday morning and take the ferry across that night. This will get us to Liverpool on Thursday where we'll stay the weekend, see his church, take his Mass, take advantage of that special indulgence. Then down to London by train on Monday. I'm thrilled to bits!

Homer has sent me a to-do list. 'You must go to Harrods for tea and cucumber sandwiches. Say hello to the teddy bears. Then, you must go to Floris and buy yourself a big bottle of eau de cologne.'

He even enclosed a traveller's cheque for $20 to pay for it. But he also sent a warning. 'Just because the good Father wears black does not mean he has good taste.'

The ferry isn't glamorous at all. It's packed to the gills with everyone smoking and drinking. And Mammie's unhappy Father Bob doesn't spring for cabins. He says he's happy to sit up in the bar all night. So she and I have no recourse but to settle down in the lounge with a packet of Digestive biscuits, a few Cadbury bars and tea.

Mammie crumples up on a bench and falls asleep. But I'm not sleepy. I'm hopping out of my skin with excitement. I go out on deck and look into the dark. I, Alice Marie Carey, am finally sailing to the land of William Shakespeare, Noel Coward and the Queen!

Yet from the moment the docks come in view, I can see that Liverpool looks sort of sad, even with the funny 'liver birds' Father Bob points out on top of the Custom House. On the drive to Bootle, all we see is vacant lot after vacant lot, crumbling brick houses, wallflowers and stray dogs. Mammie says it's not fully recovered from being bombed in the war.

Then suddenly, there it is. Smack in the middle of a vacant corner lot is a green Nissen hut with a large sign proclaiming: Our Lady of Walsingham.

Mammie's shocked.

Father Bob's thrilled.

'Green, eh Alice. For Ireland.'

'Of course,' says Mammie.

'No Union Jack here,' says Father Bob.

The presbytery is worse. In Carrigeen, he never stopped talking about his 'smashing new house'. Can't he see this is a two-up two-down terraced house in Bootle? Bootle, for God's sake, wherever that is.

'Near the race track,' he bleats. 'The Grand National, eh Alice?'

But Bootle isn't Liverpool and Liverpool isn't England. Only London is England. We're trapped and that's the truth.

Hefty Joan, Father Bob's housekeeper, greets us at the front door. She gives Mammie a squeeze. She calls me 'ducky'. *Bang*! goes the kettle. Out come the bikkies. Welcome to England.

In less than a minute, Mammie and Joan are thicker than thieves. You should see the two of them acting like Father Bob's handmaidens! Worse, they're happy. Happy, to be divvying up duties they'll perform for the nearest thing they have next to God.

Joan does his laundry. 'Missus, I know me starch. That I do.' Mammie makes his bed and tidies his room. Then she starts in telling old Joan that the General taught her all there is to know about bedmaking. She does it like they do in the army. Several times a day we walk over to 'Our Lady', and each time Father Bob has some new revelation for us.

'Alice M'rie, now here's a surprise for you. I'll bet you don't know whom "Our Lady" has on board? George Harrison's mother, that's who. I've met George on occasion. He's a good lad … I didn't know he was Catholic.'

Then Mammie asks, 'Who is George Harrison? Is he Rex's son?'

There are no holy statues in the Nissen hut. But there are Stations of the Cross and about fifty folding chairs. That's it. Father Bob doesn't seem to mind. I don't think he sees what I see at all.

I'm shocked that Jesus is living in a hut. Yet the red light is on day and night saying Jesus is in residence. But instead of residing on a marble altar, 'Jesus of Bootle' has parked his shepherd's crook on an old kitchen table covered with a white cloth.

'We're planning a bazaar to get a proper altar. Mrs Harrison, Louise I call her, said George might lend a hand. Maybe he could come by and sing us a few songs like that one you like, Alice M'rie – "I Wanna Hold Your Hand".'

'But Bob,' asks Mammie in true despair. 'Why have ye no electricity?'

'We don't need any. We do all our services in daylight.'

'Even Christmas?' say I.

'We haven't had a Christmas yet.'

With nothing left to say, we walk down to the shops for a shin of beef, spuds, onions, a cabbage and a kidney. Joan is planning a Lancashire hotpot.

* * *

That Saturday morning with Father Bob off at the track, Mammie and Joan clean out his study. It's a smelly old place with ashtrays piled with butts, jars of pomade, a bottle of Jameson and tattered copies of *The Field*.

Mammie gets me to pitch in with the promise of pictures of India Father Bob took when he was an RAF chaplain during the War.

I dust around a bit while she starts tidying the top shelves of the bookcase. Raymond Chandler, *The Silver Chalice*, *National Geographic* and *Punch*. She's fretting about himself coming back and finding us rummaging about.

Joan says Father Bob spends the whole day at the track. Then she has the nerve to say, 'Alice M'rie, why don't you go to Confession to your Uncle? I'm sure he wouldn't be hard on the sins of a young girl.'

I pay her no mind and start looking at the snaps. A lot of them have a pretty Indian lady standing with Father

Bob in front of a chapel, in a jeep and in front of the Taj Mahal. His arm is always around her. She's wearing a sari. He's in khakis without his Roman collar. Younger. Thinner. Smoking. Same shiny black hair, parted in the middle.

'Are you enjoying the pictures?' asks Mammie floating by.

'Aren't they lovely?' asks Joan. 'Father has that fine woman with him.'

Mammie bends down for a look. She sees what I'm looking at and grabs the box of snaps and puts it back on the shelf.

'That's enough of that. Bob can't expect us to look after him. Isn't he the messy one now?'

'He is that,' says Joan.

'He must learn to live with his mess,' says Mammie.

'Let's have a cup of tea,' says Joan.

I've got to get out of here and get to London. But that's only part of it. There's more. More, I tell you.

* * *

The green hut did Mammie in. It's not what she wanted for her brother. She's up most of the night sitting at the window, reading crime pages by lamplight. When morning rolls around, she's already up, dressed and raring to help Joan. I have a sleep-in as I'm a little queasy from the Lancashire hotpot.

I hear the door open.

'Mammie?'

It's Father Bob in his bathrobe. I get up and grab a sweater from the chair to cover myself. Yet I don't know why. After all, he is my uncle. He is a priest – a man I've written letters to all my life. And I'm clothed. I have on a white cotton nightgown.

'Alice M'rie, I'm so sorry. I was dreaming … and stumbled into … I'm so sorry.'

'That's okay, Father Bob. Mammie said you were at a meeting.' But he makes no motion to leave. 'Mammie's expecting me downstairs, I've got to get dressed.'

'Of course. Well then, Alice M'rie, I took a look at you in Saint Mary's yesterday. What a fine woman you're turning out to be.'

'Oh thanks.'

'Now, how about a hug?'

'Sure.'

With that, my Uncle comes toward me, puts his arms around me, kisses me hard and sticks his smelly cigarette-tongue in my mouth. He won't let go. And his squeeze hurts. I can feel something hard through his old green dressing gown. I don't know what it is, but it feels like a sin. Mustering every drop of strength I have, I push Father Bob away and he comes crashing down on the bed.

'Alice M'rie, are ye all right?' I hear Mammie's step in the downstairs hall. 'Did ye fall out of bed?'

'No, no, I'm grand. A wasp came in the window. I swatted at it and tripped.'

In a flash Mammie's up the stairs and Father Bob hides behind the drapes. I run to the window and start whooshing out the imaginary wasp.

Mammie surveys the situation from the doorway.

'You should have seen it, Mammie. It was huge.'

'Did it sting you?'

'Not really.'

'Alice M'rie, ye made such a clunk. Ye've got to stop eating those sweeties.'

I can see Father Bob's slippers peeking out from the drapes. Mammie goes to the window, looks out, then starts straightening up the bed.

I'm afraid to start up a chat that'll keep her here.

All I want to do is wash out my mouth. I'm not sure if the smell of Sweet Afton that's lingering in the air belongs to me or my nightdress or Father Bob. I hope Mammie doesn't smell it and think I'm smoking.

'Well then, Bob says we'd best start packing for London. We're off tomorrow.'

Mammie leaves and Father Bob pulls the drapes aside. He's pinned to the spot with embarrassment. We just stand there. I tell him to go into the loo and flush.

'The noise'll cover you going to your room.'

Father Bob leaves. I brush my teeth till my gums bleed. I can't tell Mammie. It'd kill her.

12

Sadness & London

I now call him Bob. True to his word he takes us to London. Down by train, lunch included – pork chops and silence – gagged by our secret. Then he starts reciting nursery rhymes.

> *To London*
> *To London to buy a fat pig.*
> *Home again, home again*
> *Jiggidy Jig.*

Then he coughs up a laugh and lights up another fag. It doesn't matter to me that it's raining when we arrive at St Pancras station. I'm just glad to be here. Bob is in his element. He waltzes us around Piccadilly Circus. 'See there, Alice M'rie, the statue of Eros.'

Ha! Mammie hasn't a clue what he's going on about. Old bastard must be terrified I'll tell. But I can't tell her, and he knows it. What can I say? Oh Mammie, I'm sorry to report that your brother the priest popped into the room a few mornings ago and stuck his tongue down my throat.

Committed a mortal sin, Bob did. Who will he go to for Confession? Ha? That's what I think. What could he say? He'll have to confess to himself. And he'll get himself off the hook, too.

Guilt and Atonement must be twins. Bob plies me with Kit-Kats, Cadbury's, Black Magic, Turkish Delights and Fry's Creams. Purses, booklets, bookmarks, books, scarves, any postcard I want. Oh, but the smell of him makes me sick. I'll never walk next to that man again, ever.

There he is, trotting up ahead like a scoutmaster waving his brolly, whilst Mammie and I bring up the rear. How could I have ever held hands with that big black blob? That beetle! That tub of lard! That priest!

We're at St Paul's Cathedral looking at the famous life-sized portrait of Jesus knocking at a door. Gazing at it I imagine Jesus scolding me. He sounds just like Bob.

'Well then, my child, holding hands with a priest, eh, and of your own free will too? You committed a sin. You let your uncle, a priest – my right-hand man – hold your *haaaaaand*. You let him hold your hand.

'You lured him on with all your foolish thoughts of romance. "Some enchanted evening you will see a stranger across a crowded room." Well Missy, wishes can come true.'

'No, no, Jesus. I didn't. I don't know how to lure anybody on. 'Tis he's the priest. He's the adult. I'm the child.'

Mammie sees me staring at Jesus.

'Alice M'rie, why are ye looking at that picture?'

'I dunno.'

'And what's happened with ye and Bob? He says ye don't like him any more … and you're calling him Bob!'

Good! I got her goat. And for a moment I feel OK.

We walk the streets single file. Bob up ahead with his patent leather hair, pack of fags, nicotine-stained fingers, clerical collar, fat knees, and phony English-ese. How I hate him and his *Cheerio*! Cheerio then, Ta. Luv. I say Alice M'rie, how 'bout a fag? How 'bout a kiss?

And his table manners, slicing off the top of a soft-boiled egg with a one-two hit of his knife. Bang! Lining up peas on the tines of his fork – one, two, three, four, five – then smashing them into a wad of spuds, a hit of gravy and cramming them all in his mouth at the same time. The same mouth that transforms bread and wine into Christ's body and blood. The same mouth that kissed me.

There he is singing up ahead in the rain. And he's no Gene Kelly.

London Bridge is falling down, falling down, falling down. London Bridge is falling down, my fair lady.

Mammie and I trail behind. It's raining hard. Drilling down. Nothing stops Bob. Up the Mall: 'there's the Palace.' Down to Knightsbridge: 'there's the park.' Then the fool forgets his bowler in the Trafalger Square loo. Oh, the holy Father takes off his hat to pee? Men are foolish old fools, all of them.

Bob scampers up Piccadilly. The rain is beating down on his bare head. And his dripping hair is hanging there, framing his face, like two dead crows. Mammie laughs and Bob says: 'I say, Alice it's not funny. That hat cost me fifty quid.'

Quid, another of his expressions. He looks like an undertaker. We go to the Ladies at Harrods and bust our guts laughing at him. I don't get to say 'hello' to the teddy bears.

We take a peek at the Tower of London and Westminster Abbey. But these don't really interest Bob. He's all fluffed up about Madame Tussaud's. The rain has stopped. It's now the hottest day London has seen since the night of the Big Fire.

He whisks us past the waxworks of the Royal Family, Churchill and The Beatles. Down, down, down we go to the Chamber of Horrors. That's why we're here. Not for me but for him! It's dark, creepy, humid and smelly.

Bob starts pointing out the finer points of execution.

'There's the guillotine. The rack. The stake. I say, Alice M'rie, it's a terrible thing the harm human beings inflict upon each other.'

Is this an apology? Is Bob confessing he's sorry to me at Madame Tussaud's?

We linger at the *tableaux vivants* with their blood-red lighting and soundtrack of cries and whimpers for hanging, boiling, flaying, burning – each method worse than the one before.

It's roasting. There's blood everywhere. Kids are screaming in terror and Mammie starts giggling away. Why, I don't know. I collapse. Right there on the floor of Madame Tussauds. There's no air. There I am on the floor wondering if Bob and I committed a sin of impurity together, and is my half Mortal or Venial? If it's Mortal,

I'll burn in Hell. If it's Venial, I'll sweat in Purgatory. I don't know what'll they do with Bob. Bet he'll give himself a dispensation.

They get me up. They get me out. They walk me to Westminster Cathedral (the Catholic one, says Bob) to sit in a coolness known only to churches in summer.

This isn't the London Homer had in mind. But it is London. I am here. I love what I see. And I'll come back. Then we return to Liverpool, where the other shoe drops.

13

Summer's End

B ob announces he wants to accompany 'the ladies' back to Ireland. Mammie's all smiles, thrilled to be having more time with him. 'Oh Bob what'll your parishioners do without you?' Do? They'll be ecstatic not to see those yellowed fingers waving the Eucharist around.

So it's back to Kerry. When the Slatterys see the Morris pull into the haggard, they're shocked. But Bob breezily says, 'I want to do something nice for Alice M'rie.'

He doesn't say what he wants to do, other than whatever it is, it's for *me*. Excitement is mounting at the Slatterys' house. Expectations are high. But I don't care a bit about that. Just like before, every day is the same, beginning with 'The Ballad of Mary Falvey'. Whatever

Bob's planning, I won't sit by him at the table, nor next to him in the Morris.

'The honeymoon's over,' laughs Dave.

On Sunday I tell them I'm sick. I don't go to Bob's Mass. Feck his indulgence. I've enough special indulgences to last me a lifetime.

I stay in bed looking at the Paps. I'm trying to read Eugene O'Neill's *Long Day's Journey Into Night*, because Homer said there'd be a moment when I'd feel the need to read another Irish family drama.

It's nice to be alone. It's a beautiful day, but I don't care. I want to be back in New York on Lexington Avenue where I feel at home. I wonder what Homer's doing. It's Sunday. Bet he's walking around the Village eating pastries.

Miss D. is having lunch on the terrace in the country. The General is mixing drinks under that umbrella of his, proclaiming *Ginder Ale*.

Yet I'm in the country too. Ireland *is* Country. I hang my head out the window. There's the road. There are the cows. There's D.D. down by the stream with them. Down a-ways are the Killarney churches with everyone praying away. Ireland on a Sunday – a day of rest – no one rests ever in Carrigeen.

I hear Dave Slattery's booted foot on the stair.

'Alice Maria … '

That's how he pronounces it – Maria.

'Yer uncle has a proposal.'

I like Dave. He hasn't a clue.

Bob is standing in the kitchen under the picture of the Sacred Heart, nursing a neat Paddy. Mammie is sitting by the fire, looking quite bleak.

'Alice M'rie, would you like to visit your father's ancestral home?'

'I've never thought about it.'

'It would complete the family picture for you. This is why I came back to Carrigeen, for you to put your father in the picture. It's the least I can do.'

'Mammie, what do you think?'

'I want nothing at all to do with it.'

Bob lights up an Afton. Mammie straightens her hat and goes out to the haggard to stare at the cows. I give a scad eye to Jesus up there on the Holy Shelf, his fingers touching that bloody wound. While here in the kitchen another wound is opening up.

*　*　*

We're set to return to New York on Friday and Mammie's stalling. She doesn't want to go to Coomacullin. Yet Bob insists we must see the house where Carey was born.

Dave suggests a taxi. But Bob's adamant. He wants to drive us himself. All I want is to get it over with. I have to get back to glamour. Pissing into a basin for two months is enough to make a girl desperate.

Bob suggests Wednesday.

Around noon we get into the Morris and Bob asks Mammie which way to turn because he has forgotten the map.

'Over there, on the other side of that,' says Mammie, pointing a gloved finger to the Paps.

Bob takes off at his steady thirty miles an hour, Mammie in front, me in back. Next to me on the seat are an iced barmbrack and a bottle of Paddy – offerings for Carey's brother's widow and her daughter, who is my cousin.

'Mammie, what're their names?'

'Kathleen's the mother. I don't know the daughter's.'

We look like we're dressed for lunch at the Waldorf. Mammie all decked out in her tipsy soufflé hat, me in my blazer with the crest signifying nothing.

We head towards Killarney to buy a map. Bob comes back to the car with a regional map and a book for me, *The Great Hunger*. What he doesn't remember is that he sent a copy to Astoria years ago.

We chug out of Killarney and proceed east. There's nothing left to say. Bob and I have not a drop of palaver left. After about twenty minutes on the Kilgarvin road, the landscape changes from pastoral to rocky.

We drive into the hills. Fallen boulders form a gauntlet. The windows are getting dusty. There are no houses around. This is not the landscape coveted by tourists. We drive on till the road dead ends on a muddy goat path, going straight up a steep hill.

'Alice, is this the right way?'

'How would I know?'

'But Mammie, did you not go visiting there when you and Carey were courting?'

'I've never been up here at all.'

We get out of the car. Bob walks away to 'relieve' himself. Mammie and I look up the hill. But it isn't a hill. It's a mountain – a huge, rocky, dusty mountain with nary a bit of green to dress it up.

Bob returns.

'I say, ladies, do you have to pay a visit to Mrs Murphy? Better here than there.' And he gestures upward.

I hate him. Who does he think he is, telling my Mammie to pee on a rock? She'd rather die. Me too. And I really have to go.

Bob revs up the Morris and Mammie takes off her gloves. Then she puts them back on, and takes them off again. I see myself in the rear-view mirror. My face is oily.

My eyes are puffy. My bun is so squeezed on my head I look like I'm bald.

'Oh dear,' says Bob, clutching the gearstick and jerking it back and forth.

'Now Bob …' says Mammie, putting her now-gloved hand on his black-suited arm. Suddenly the gears seem to explode from Bob fiddling with them. His hand rapidly pushes into one gear, then the next and the next and we assault the hill. The cake's flung on the floor. The icing cracks.

'Jesus, Mary and sweet Saint Joseph!' hoots Bob as the Morris jerks forward, rolls back and stalls again.

Mammie's face is shiny, moist, red and hot. She takes out her compact for a quick dust up. Bob drags on his Afton. He wipes his brow with a large linen handkerchief with the initials *Rev. RS* embroidered in red in the corner.

Mammie reminds him that *poor* Mollie embroidered it. Bob says, 'Damned hard this road. We didn't have hills like this in the Punjab. Shall we have another go?'

The wheels are spinning in the mud. The air is sharp. Bob eases his foot off the brake and whisks into another gear. The car spins sharply around and the bottle of Paddy smashes against the door.

I jump out. Mammie too, while Bob eases out on his side.

'These are some hills … eh, Alice M'rie?'

I'm terrified and I scream: 'We could've been killed. No one would find us up here, ever, ever. Mammie, the fool can't drive.'

I give her a look I regret to this day. A look that indicated she is She and I am I. We are no longer *we*.

'Alice M'rie, apologise to Father Bob.'

'I will not. If the two of you are so intent on me seeing Carey's home, we should've gotten a hackney who knows how to drive.'

'Now, Alice,' says Bob, dropping the M'rie. 'What would you like me do? I don't want to ruin your holiday.'

I say nothing. Mammie and Bob stand there glaring at me. I walk away. It's so bleak. Sheep come and go. There's not a house to be seen. And here are Mammie and I, all dolled up with no place to go. I start to cry.

'I want to go back to New York.'

Bob hands Mammie his handkerchief. She daubs her face then takes a tube of Elizabeth Arden's 'Stop Red!' lipstick from her handbag and daubs it on her lips. She hands the handkerchief to me.

'Wipe yer face, Alice M'rie.'

Our sweat comingles. I look up at the mountain. 'Is that where he really came from?' I do not say Daddy, Father, or Carey and neither do they.

'It is a long way up, and the cake and whiskey are ruined,' says Bob.

'Yes,' says Mammie. 'We wouldn't want to try again and damage your new car.'

We drive back to Killarney in silence, leaving the broken cake and glass on the mountain.

* * *

Big plans are afoot for our last night. Dave says that years ago when someone left home, those left behind had a wake in the West Room to say goodbye. Everyone stayed up till dawn, dancing and singing. Then they sang the person down the road to America, never ever to return. But not us ... Mammie vows we'll return next year and the next, and the one after that.

Bob slipped away to Bootle at the crack of dawn. We didn't hear him go. Mammie says it'd break his heart to say goodbye, so he just left. I feel like the noose of fear has been loosened from around my neck.

We take the bus to Killarney for a last look around. We're buying a leg of lamb and Mammie's going to cook it the way she does for Miss D. She's also buying a pound of Nescafe for Irish coffee and a pint of double cream for the whipped topping. I buy my last lot of Cadbury's.

She buys Dave a bottle of Paddy, Mary Falvey a bottle of Yardley cologne and the lads winter jumpers.

We visit the old haunts. The lanes. The cobbler. The butcher. The Arbutus. Mammie lights a candle at the Cathedral to insure the *Mauretania* won't sink.

We drop by the Sullivans where Haulie gives me a gold wool Aran sweater – gold, mind, not your ordinary white. We promise to write. And he gives me a tentative hug.

'Ye're th'real article, Alice M'rie', he says as I walk away wiping tears from my eyes.

Dinner in the West Room is delicious. Mary Falvey has set the table with the good china. I sit under my favourite picture of the three blind girls and look around at all the old snaps of the Slatterys. New snaps of Mammie and me and Bob on this trip will soon join them.

There's Guinness and Paddy and Dubonnet all around, and a Coca-Cola for me. The skin of the roast lamb crackles. Mammie's made a *jus de glace*. No doughy gravy here. She's even decorated the swedes with a brown sugar glaze. The spuds, picked an hour before being boiled, lie on a large blue willow-pattern platter slathered with sweet butter and salt.

When a cake is brought out Dave proclaims: 'Ye'll never eat th'likes of this in New York, Alice Maria.'

He's right. Mary Falvey's cream cake, with blackberries I picked up the lane, is as light as a feather. Through the haze of Sweet Afton, order had been restored.

Robert brings down the Victrola. We crank it up to play *My Fair Lady* and I do my not-so-good imitation of Julie Andrews. D.D. makes Irish coffee. Mary Falvey settles in front of the fire and announces, 'Th'whishkey through th'whipped cream is killin' me.' Then she starts crying. 'O Alish, please God, ye'll come *Home* again soon.'

Dave cranks up the Victrola again, puts on *Peter Pan* and we all sit still while Mary Martin sings: '*My child, my very own, don't be afraid, you're not alone.*'

Mammie does the washing-up and I walk out to the apple orchard. I feel sad that I didn't love *Home* like Mammie hoped I would. Saying, 'I want to go back to New York' up there in Coomacullin killed her.

I go up to the bedroom and look out at the Paps. It's near midnight, at the end of a lingering August twilight in the west of Ireland in the 1960s. Downstairs I can hear Mammie singing.

> *We'll build a dear little nest*
> *Somewhere out in the West*
> *And let the rest of the world go by.*

I feel sick. I don't want to use the 'po'. I've got to go outside. In the apple orchard under a full moon I vomit. My period's begun and I'm bleeding. I cry. My summer vacation is over. I grew up.

14

'Penny Lane'

On our way back from the Skelligs Geoffrey and I take David LaGreca to the church of St James the Apostle, just outside our village. In *A Parish History*, published for its 200th anniversary, a historian described the view. '*To see a sunset on that harbour of a summer's evening would cast a ray of light upon one's bosom and that would make it look like a pathway to heaven.*'

And it is.

We start poking around the old cemetery, reading aloud eighteenth-century headstones. The Shannons who once owned our house are buried here. Suddenly, who should suddenly appear by the stile but Sallie Keating.

'Sallie,' I say, running over to her and giving her a hug. 'You must meet our friend, David LaGreca. He's heard all about you.'

'Sure girl, why would he even hear about me?'

'Because you're fabulous.'

Sallie laughs shyly, *fabulous* not being a word in her vocabulary.

LaGreca sidles up to Sallie. 'You remind me of my mother,' he says giving her a hug.

'Has she died?

'A few years ago.'

'Well then, I'll give you a hug. And she does. 'I'm here to look at my grave … I'm going right there.' Sallie points to a grassy plot by the church's front door. 'I'll miss nothing there, nothing at all. They'll all have to pass by me to get in here, heaven as well.'

As we continue reading headstones, Sallie picks weeds from her future plot.

Later on that evening, chicken in the Aga and wine in hand, the three of us walk our old laneway. LaGreca can't get over Sallie.

'She *is* fabulous. She could lecture a theology class on the spiritual connection she's made between being alive and being dead. Some of the AIDS guys we saw die made the same connection and died peacefully. They just crossed over the bridge.'

Peter Pan pops into my head, and I tell David that as Peter was about to walk the plank he said: 'Death must be an awfully big adventure.'

'Are you putting Sallie Keating, Peter Pan and all the AIDS guys in the same boat?'

'In a way. I remember Scott on his last day on earth, morphine drip in his arm easing his way across the rainbow bridge. He was completely at peace. I don't think I could be that way.'

'Not without a morphine drip.'

We go for another another poke around the Big House and wind up in the West Room. I start telling LaGreca about its connection with the dead, only to be reminded by Geoffrey's eyes that I'm in danger of killing the conversation.

Silence descends as we stand outside the old front door with its rusted brass knob, and glass transom that illuminated every person who ever entered this house.

LaGreca breaks the silence. 'When did your mother die?'

'End of the sixties.'

'And your father?'

'End of the eighties.'

'Alice doesn't talk about either death,' says Geoffrey. 'It's as if they never happened.'

But as I look over my shoulder into my own West Room, Mammie's death returns.

* * *

Through the whole of Mammie's funeral, The Beatles song 'Penny Lane' plays in my head. It's my distraction from Carey while we sit by ourselves in the front row of the Immaculate Conception waiting for Mass to begin. It's a Thursday in December and *'Penny Lane is in my ears and in my eyes.'*

Shifting my legs from the nearness of Carey's knees, my eyes wander around this sandstone horror, and I think about why I fled from Astoria to New York only four months before.

'There beneath the blue suburban skies.'

Two days ago my Mammie was clipped by a hit-and-run driver while she was dashing home to make Carey's morning tea, after cooking up a fry for two old Irish pensioners who lived down the way. She did things like that. She'd take on the damnedest people, as if she didn't have enough to do tending Miss D.

Ten to ten. O'Shea, the funeral director next door, hustled the mourners out too early and into here. Bet he has another coffin waiting in the wings.

'O'Shea gives a great send-off. Better him than them Guinzos down the way.' That's Carey's opinion. Now he really knows.

In her pink suit she is. Her Jackie Kennedy suit, without the pillbox hat. I picked out her eggshell-white straw hat, with little beauty marks strewn across the veil. But O'Shea said no.

'Hats aren't worn in coffins.'

'Mammie wore hats all the time.'

'It just isn't done.'

So she isn't wearing a hat. Nor is she carrying her pocket book, or wearing gloves, just a rosary twined around her fingers.

So toil worn for me
Ah, bless you and keep you,
Mother Macree.

Hateful Irish-American sentimentality.

I'm sitting in a church I'll never return to, whilst Mammie is laid out next door in a cheap plywood coffin covered in Mother Mary blue damask.

I could have knelt down and said a prayer, damn it. I could have gone in to take a look at her, to see if the suit looked all right. But I didn't. I couldn't. I didn't want to see her dead. I spent the wake in O'Shea's office, with my girlfriend Dianne, devouring a box of chocolates we found in his desk.

Wasn't it only a week ago Mammie and I were looking at the giant Rockefeller Center Christmas tree? I met her at Miss D.'s. She said she wanted to walk over and see the tree.

Walking over to 5th Avenue she was going on about a wake she'd just gone to at O'Shea's, and I was telling her I never again want to look at anyone dead in a coffin. I'd seen too many already. Mammie was laughing. 'Ye go for the gossip,' she said.

I should have checked to see if the cheap coffin really looked cheap. Cheap wood rots faster than mahogany.

Two to ten. O'Shea and the pallbearers are late. They should be in the back of the church by now. Blame it on the solstice. Today's the shortest day of the year.

Sitting behind Carey and me are pews full of weeping neighbours, all eyes glued on us. They're burning a hole in the back of my head. Mrs Scott. Mrs Jackson. Mrs Trainor. Mrs Kelly. I can smell Mrs Donovan's Camels, Lily McCann's snuff. The cold of the Mac holds the smells.

Miss D.'s here too. I smell her Blue Grass perfume. Bet she's wearing her little mink and her little thrup'ny-bit heels. I'd like to know who made her tea this morning. Someone'll have to learn to boil water.

A Janus image they were, Mammie and Miss D. Connected by airs. Set apart by class and money. Yet I don't think Mammie felt an iota of resentment. It was almost as if it were her job on this earth to minister to Miss D. Now it's over. No one can ever replace my Mammie. Miss D. knows it. They all know it.

The General is here too, all decked out in his uniform and war medals. That'll cause a stir among the populace. But it's Homer who runs the show. Even the most miserly funeral is a show. If I turn around halfway I can see him standing in the back greeting people. Homer lives for style and ritual. He called me up at six this morning with a style tip.

'Dwa-linggggg … you must err on the side of chic for Big Alice's High Mass. The day will be warm enough for your peach coat.'

And I'm wearing it. I'm the only one not dressed in black or mink.

Now Mammie's dead. Dead to begin with like Jacob Marley. I never really got that until now – 'dead to begin with'. Killed in the midst of doing a good deed.

If I had a dime for every fruit cake she gave old ladies, or Sunday supplements she mailed back to Ireland, or bags of groceries she lugged for sick neighbours, or the hundreds of nylons she washed by hand in the basin for Miss D., I'd have enough money to send her body back to Ireland. She might have wanted that.

'I don't know. She didn't say ... How I long for yesterday.'

People will always remember that she died in the street by the gas tanks. Now that's a sight that sticks. Legs askew. Hat off. Spilt milk. Don't cry after. Always helping others, Carey who never appreciated her, sometimes me and never herself.

Sitting beside Carey right now in this pew is the closest I've been to him in years. Mrs Pelleteri is waving at me, pointing at my coat. Yes, it is nice. I bet she's made a connection that Mammie's in pink and I'm in peach.

'And all the people that come and go / Stop and say Hello.'

Penny Lane. Liverpool. Killarney. Astoria. Fire Island. New York. All the same, they are. *Home* ... Alice M'rie. John Lennon said The Beatles were more famous than Jesus Christ. But God is dead. To have my Mammie die in the street like that ...

Broke her heart I did. She stayed in bed the whole day I moved out. She knew she'd be stuck in Astoria with Carey. Oh, we patched it up a bit. She came down to my one-roomed apartment in the Village a few times with corn muffins and tuna fish. But things were never the same again.

Three minutes past ten. Maybe it's all a joke. I bet my Mammie's gotten up out of that cheap coffin and she's across the street banging on the Deutsch Brothers door, looking for lamb chops. But she's not. The Deutsch Brothers are standing there in the back – Dave, Joe and Jack, all wearing yarmulkes. They've closed the store in Mammie's honour.

Members of the Rosary Society line the aisle awaiting her coffin.

The family that prays together stays together.

The Careys didn't.

The Careys couldn't.

We didn't even go to Mass together.

D.D. Carey is mute. He must know Mammie took the back way down by the gasworks as a shortcut home, to avoid him seeing her coming from the pensioners, avoid his judgment and possibly his hand.

He whispers that the pensioners rang O'Shea's last night to say they'd be praying the Mass at home, along with Father Lyons. They said 'We'll get her Mammie into heaven, don't you worry.'

Everyone's standing. It's really happening. Mammie is not buying chops. Father Lyons is in position. The organ is wheezing out the Mass for the Dead.

Black was Mammie's favourite colour. Maybe she should be wearing her black suit, not that pink one. Dreary music. An overture from one of Miss D.'s shows would be better.

The Rosarians, led by that old whited sepulchre Mrs Bray, turn and face the door. I just yelled at the old bitch in the back of the church when she tried to hug me. Shouldn't have done that. All she did was remind me of the importance of the Rosary.

Yet all the rosaries in the world didn't stop that car from hitting Mammie.

Ah, Mrs Bray'll chalk it up to grief. 'You miss your Mammie,' she said, as Homer pulled me away. 'We'll say the Rosary for her.'

It's not grief. It's anger. My Mammie didn't give two shites about the rosary, or novenas, or any of that hocus-pocus going on up there. My Mammie cared about properly ironed hems. Red lipstick. Hats. My posture. Tuna sandwiches. A proper pot of tea with honey in a blue pitcher, and that I'd turn out to be a lady. A Lady. Not a greenhorn. Not a narrowback. But a Lady, a New Yorker.

And I am a lady wearing a peach coat from Bergdorf Goodman. Bergdorf's, I tell you, not Bloomingdale's. Not Macy's. But Bergdorf's on 5th Avenue.

Mrs Bray gives the signal. The Rosarians raise their arms to heaven. Rosary beads jingling, fingers touching.

Suddenly, the world I know changes utterly as I stand to watch the coffin of my Mammie, Alice Slattery Carey, slide up the aisle on her way to cross the bridge to heaven.

* * *

A great silence descends as Geoffrey and I and LaGreca wend our way back to the stable. As LaGreca pours wine he says, 'Guys, I figured out what you should name this place – "Faileth Not". I saw that carved on one of the old tombstones today. "Faileth Not" is what you guys are all about.'

15

Queen of the Fields

By the time LaGreca left, Geoffrey and I were nearing the end of our stay. Every day we hoovered, and every day the silt returned. We were still sleeping on the floor. I was still walking with a stoop. And we hadn't made love.

In an attempt to do something nice for ourselves, we drove up to Cork city to spend a night in Moore's Hotel. But when we got there, and after taking hot showers that lasted an hour, all we had the energy to do was lie in bed, hold each other and rub our iron-stiff necks.

Then a week or so before our return to New York, I heard a faint meow in the middle of the night. It seemed to be coming from the Hermitage. Geoffrey heard it as well. Neither of us told the other. For what would we do with a cat in Ireland?

I love cats. Starting with Mitzi, I've never been without one. Yet Ireland's strict quarantine law made it impossible to bring an animal back and forth from another country. Any cat we'd take on would have to stay right here.

Meows persisted.

We ignored them.

Then I relented and went outside.

'Cat ...?' I said.

'Meow,' said Cat.

From behind the Hermitage, up popped a jet-black kitten with lettuce-green eyes. And in a twinkling of those eyes, we were hers.

We had but a week to know her, to tame her, to love her. Were it a month we could have done this gradually. Out came bowls of milk, titbits of bacon, smidgens of chicken. Sheila said farm cats love bread soaked in milk. So did this one. Pretty soon Cat was in the house, on the couch and on our mattress.

'That's good luck, girl,' proclaimed Sallie. 'A black cat showing up out of the blue.'

'Is it a gift from the fairies?' I ask. 'That's what I want to know.' Sallie looks away, so as not to offend the possibility.

We couldn't keep calling her Cat. So we named her Thomasina, after the brilliant young girl in Tom Stoppard's *Arcadia,* a play I love.

The name *Thomasina* confused everyone. Try as I might to explain that Stoppard's Thomasina is a mathematical genius in love with her tutor, who upon her tragic death, winds up his days living in a hermitage, I failed dismally. Yet it was only fitting the cat that turned up on our Hermitage would be named Thomasina.

For the week we had her, we loved her to bits and wept at the thought of abandoning her. But we had to. On our last morning, as we drove down the laneway, lit only by the morning star, a small black cat stood guard on the Hermitage – Thomasina, our bright particular star.

She could go in and out through an open window. The Aga would keep the house warm. The Keatings would feed her. And she'd not be wandering the roads. It was all we could do. It was the best we could do. If she stayed around, we'd not see her again till we returned for Christmas.

* * *

When we settled back in New York it dawned on us just how difficult it would be to live in Ireland *and* in New York. On Fire Island we knew the entertainer Peter Allen, who'd set everyone laughing by saying he was 'bicoastal'. Peter's ease in living on two coasts captured our imaginations. Now, in our own way, so were we. Yet, actually *living* in the stable gave Geoffrey and I a wake-up call on how skewed our lives were fast becoming.

You'd think we'd see the difference between going out to Fire Island every weekend, and having to plan months ahead to take a plane to Ireland. But we hadn't. Then again, had we thought about how complicated it would be, we might never have bought a house there.

We were proud that we achieved our goal of buying a house in Ireland. But at the end of the day, a stable is a stable. The Big House, the house we crawled in the window of, the house we fell in love with, remained derelict on the ridge. We hadn't a clue what to do with it.

To restore the Big House properly, to beautifully decorate it in true nineteenth-century standards we'd have to give up Fire Island. We could no longer maintain the fantasy of living there, New York, *and* Ireland.

A decision of Heart vs. Purse was made. 'Magic Flute' would have to go. Not only did we feel unfaithful to our old love, we felt we were letting down our neighbours who were living with, and dying from, AIDS.

Fire Island seemed to have changed overnight. Back when all things were beautiful, when we heard a police siren in the middle of the night indicating that someone had to be taken off the island, we'd rush out to see who it was and if we could help. Now, we'd go on with what we were doing. We had got so used to sirens and helicopters, we didn't want to know who the next person was being taken off, much less who had died in his home, or was near death.

Survival guilt riddled our lives.

From the gardens of 'Magic Flute' we could see people passing by on the walk. When I'd spy a pal newly disfigured from Kaposi Sarcoma lesions, I found myself walking around the gardens kicking sand, crying out: 'It's not fair. It's not fair.'

Once Beauty surrounded the island. Now Death enveloped house after house. Even sadder, residents began to get bitter that this disease no one knew anything about had turned Paradise into Hell. Nothing would ever be the same. And so, Geoffrey and I decided to keep our happy memories intact by leaving.

When neighbours greeted me on the boardwalk, I found I was already missing them, even ones I never really liked. Islanders to whom I only gave a nod of the head were now part of the tapestry I was willing to sacrifice, for a tapestry yet to be woven.

On clear autumn nights, Geoffrey and I would stand on the top deck of 'Magic Flute' looking up at the stars and across the ocean.

'Ireland,' we'd say, pointing east.

'Home,' I'd say, pointing downstairs.

We knew we had to drop hints about leaving. Treasonous! Two healthy people leaving while others are dying. When I told my pal Dottie Cox, she flung her body against our gate in a dramatic gesture.

'You can't!' she said. 'You cannot leave here.' Then she grabbed me. And with tears in her eyes we just stood there clinging to each other.

* * *

All that autumn, worry was my constant companion. I never stopped worrying about how we'd tend to four acres, Thomasina, the weather, the Big House and the stable. Money was tight.

Our hoped-for August idyll that turned into a nineteen-day reality check made it clear that if we wanted our property to be as beautiful as what we saw in *Country Life*, we'd have to do much of the work ourselves.

When Geoffrey and I moved in together in the 1970s, all we did was merge his few sticks of furniture with mine to make a home. 'Magic Flute' came to us fully furnished (as do most houses on Fire Island). But that suited us because it was all antiques. Even now, we never buy anything new. Everything comes from flea markets and *junque* shops. But what would we do in Ireland? Beyond dealing with Frank of Drimoleague, we hadn't a clue.

16

Ringfort & City

Our Christmas plan was to get rid of the grey and paint the inside of 'Faileth Not'. What we were not ready for was the coldest winter in living memory.

We had not installed heating, because we truly believed radiators would destroy the integrity of the stable. So it was impossible to keep the place warm. Happy to be warmed only by Aga and fireplace, Geoffrey and I were eager to be on our way back to *our* home in Ireland. When the plane touched down in Cork, and Santa Claus came over to wish me Happy Christmas, I was thrilled to bits and raring to go.

As we drove up the lane, Thomasina greeted us with open paws. Each day was more beautiful than the last.

The fields had turned sage green and crunched underfoot. The pond froze and the moss became crispy and fragile. According to Met Éireann, this was an Ireland no one had ever seen before. We were so happy.

On our way through London, we had bought a gently worn green velvet Victorian chair that Aer Lingus let us bring on as cargo. We also brought over many vials of lime-wash colour pigments to be mixed by hand on site – just like they'd have been in the nineteenth century.

This was our vision: with no doors, each room opening into the next, colours would flow seamlessly from space to space. Creamy orange in the cart house would flow into the unsalted butter in the living and cooking area, while the salted butter of the boot room would flow into the chartreuse bathroom on to our lilac bedroom. Just like we'd seen in *Country Life*.

But painting was not on the cards. The persistent deep freeze in west Cork held the upper hand. Lime paint does not have the preservatives that 'Fleetwood would, would Fleetwood' has. It seized and clotted instantly, rendering it unusable. Buckets had to be brought to the dump, leaving us without a project – a state we hate being in.

Then terrible things happened.

Thomasina nearly died from a botched spaying. Our joy was so intense at seeing her we fed her and fed her the night before, and the day of, her operation. The vet should have reminded us. Then again, we should have remembered ourselves not to feed an animal about to go under anaesthesia, as it might choke from vomiting.

And Thomasina did. During and after the operation she choked, vomited and broke her stitches. Three times we had to drive in the night down the Mizen Peninsula to another village for the vet to stitch her up again. We felt so bad. Here was a kitten we had rescued that could have easily bled to death because of negligence all around.

And then, on the bitterly cold, moonlit night of the winter solstice, a Frenchwoman, Sophie Toscan du Plantier, was bludgeoned to death on the laneway of her holiday home in nearby Toormore. We'd first heard about it in Adele's in Schull while waiting to bring Thomasina home from the vet. Everyone was abuzz with gossip. Christmas took second place.

When poet John Montague wrote about Sophie for *The New Yorker* he said, 'It was the first murder in these remote parts since Civil War days.'

Sophie's death scared the daylights out of me. My hope of living a blissful, peaceful country life was broken. But what scared me even more was that in a few days I too would be a woman alone in west Cork.

Thomasina was recovering slowly. Geoffrey had to return to New York as scheduled, so I stayed on to nurse her. Part of me thought this exciting. I'd have the fire going day and night. I'd roast a chicken all for myself. Yet how could I go to the shops to buy a chicken? I don't drive.

At dawn on the feast of the Epiphany, Thomasina and I stood at the cow gate waving Geoffrey down the lane. So began my life as a woman alone in Ireland – something I hadn't counted on.

It was then I decided to hitchhike. I had no recourse but to do so. I wrote BANTRY in large letters on a piece of cardboard and walked down the lane to the road, depending on the kindness of strangers.

* * *

I returned alone in March. It was spring and Thomasina was big and well. A local painter had taken on our dream and worked with the lime pigments. It was thrilling to see our dream of flowing colours gliding together as easily as ballet dancers. As I'd go from room to room, I'd think of Kelly, a Cherry Grove pal who had died of AIDS. How he'd love to say: 'Life is meant to be lived in colour.'

Johnnie K. had returned to build front and side terraces from large flagstones we'd got in County Down.

I planted pansies, rosemary and thyme in what would become a border garden. I also painted the Dutch door vermilion to welcome the fairies, just like Sallie told me to do. The stable was finally beginning to look like home.

Thomasina and I walk the fields of an evening. It's our ritual. Without the beach to roam I've begun to think of the waving grass as sand. Light determines the time we take to the fields on our way to the ringfort behind the stable. I didn't know about ringforts until moving to west Cork. I've now read they were self-contained fortified settlements built in the early Middle Ages, high on hills so residents could see potential enemies approach from every direction.

Evening must shimmer with the expectation of night, yet be reluctant to give up the day. The land is softening. There's a hint of gold in the grass. The buds of the hawthorn are plumping up.

The temperature is a balmy 15 °C. I'm standing on the flagstone terrace looking west. Beyond Bantry Bay the mountains are getting green with the coming of spring. Thomasina is waiting. She knows the drill as she sits on the kitchen table waiting for me to pull on my wellies.

'Come on then, girl.'

My cat leaps from the table and gives herself a long, lithe stretch. Every evening we take a slightly different route to end up at our favourite place, the field at the foot of the ringfort.

Thomasina bounds out the door, heading to the top of a stile to survey the daffodils. The courtyard is a swathe of yellow daffs, old daffs – Sallie calls them *feral* – that have multiplied over the years. I have hundreds.

Thomasina and I stand on a ditch to survey the natural landscape that has taken years to evolve. Everywhere I look I see primroses, snowdrops, violets and more 'ferals'. Saying that word delights me.

Thomasina and I take to the fields. My pace is too slow, so she scoots ahead of me. Yet I can't go fast. Every step I take is a meditation on this ancient land.

We cross a field to watch neighbouring cows walk in a lazy conga line to the circular structure farmers use to place silage for cows to eat, poetically called a cow-crush. In lieu of television this is my nightly entertainment.

Thomasina leaps over a ditch Geoffrey discovered while clearing away vast thickets of dead branches overgrown with ivy and nettles. He burned back a ganglion of blackberry brambles that had obscured these stones for years. Now the ditch frames the pond. We also found two buried walls that we like to think predate our house.

The ringfort is up ahead. From a distance, it seems quite tall. Light is fading so we walk a little faster. Thomasina jumps (no, flies) then lands on an old hawthorn tree to sharpen up her claws for the fray. No fool she, my own cunning little vixen. Thomasina knows after our walk comes dinner. Maybe, if she spies a fox on the ridge for me, she'll get a sup of milk as well.

March is the best time to visit the fort. Come summer the fort will be inaccessible with its five-foot-high ferns and brambles. Last year's ferns are lying flat and soon-to-become fern fiddleheads are coming up. It is time to climb over the moat and up the bank to see the sun set. But I must be careful. Sallie told me about the fairies that live here and I must not upset them.

I stand still in the middle of this sacred space with my cat that very well may have been their gift to me.

Thomasina gets her hackles up. She puffs up to twice her size. I can feel her little heart beat proudly as she guides my eyes to something I've never seen before. On a far wall is a large red fox that disappears as soon as he senses us.

Feeling blest, for truly, this meditation is the nearest I get to prayer, Thomasina and I leave the ringfort and head for our spot, a large boulder poking up in the middle of a field. A few stars are out. All is still. All is tropic. It will rain in an hour or so. In the morning my daffodils will gleam.

Thomasina and I sit there as the last song from The Beatles' album *Abbey Road* pops into my head.

> *Once there was a way to get back homeward.*
> *Once there was a way to get back home.*

This rock. These fields. This cat. This house. This Ireland. Thomasina climbs on my lap. She seems to be purring in tune. Night is falling. It's getting hard to see. And so we go home. Thomasina to her milk, myself to the fire.

* * *

When I've been by myself for a while and need a city fix, I take the bus up to Cork city for a ramble about. I've been trying to find out if what Mammie said was true, that the Slatterys are related to Nano Nagle. I always believed her. We all believed her. It's only recently I found out this wasn't the case. Not that Mammie was lying. It was just a delusion of grandeur.

Geoffrey and I had visited the Nano Nagle Centre in Ballygriffin, where two old nuns wearing heavy cardigans, Sister Joseph and Sister Anthony (Joseph and Anthony, they called each other) talked about Nano as if they knew her personally.

'Oh she was a wild child. Wild! Wouldn't you say, Joseph? Her father used to say "Oh my Nano will be a saint, yet."'

In the kitchen, over coffee and the best fruitcake I've ever eaten, Joseph and Anthony told me Nano wasn't even on the first rung of the ladder towards Beatification.

'Girl,' said Joseph, leading me by the hand to the chapel, 'you better start praying right *now* that the Pope beatifies Nano. I'm afraid he's closing his eyes to poor old Ireland.' The Sisters said Nano's grave was on Cork's south side; and on one of my first rambles I headed straight for it.

The South Presentation Convent is hard to find. And though I could have asked for directions, I found it quite pleasurable being lost and discovering my newly adopted city on my own. After much roaming around, I came upon the convent situated up a hill on a bustling street. The gate was open, dark and unattended.

I walk up worn stone steps hugging a wall of an Ursuline convent built in 1776 and enter a walled grave-yard filled with neat rows of identical white headstones, marking the life and death of over a hundred nuns.

Right at the entrance is a crypt containing the small oak coffin of Nano Nagle. An eighteenth-century slab of granite tells her tale.

Here lie waiting, 'tis hoped, a glorious resurrection the remains of Miss Nagle ... departed this life, envied by many & regretted by all, on the 26th day of April 1784, aged 65 years.

There's a pretty view over the rooftops to the north side of the city, and the clock tower of the Church of St Anne, with its weathervane of a gold salmon. Were it a little warmer I might lie on a bench and take a nap. Everything is so green, so quiet, so comfy, so grey, so beautiful, so isolated. I don't want the aura broken by the arrival of someone wanting a chat. But I'm left alone. It's just me, Nano and, I suppose, Mammie.

I start reading the stones, postmodern in their minimalism. Here's Sister de Sales Gleeson who died this past June, sixty-two years a nun. A few red roses mark the spot. Here's Mary Connell who became Sister Mary Joseph in April 1785 and died four short months later. Rose Healy who became Sister Dorothy Clare died in 1890 at the age of twenty-three. Humble women all who followed Nano Nagle, a rich girl, who left her home to serve the poor people of Cork city.

Serve sticks in my craw. For didn't *poor* Mollie leave Carrigeen around the time of the First World War to go to England to become Sister Mary Agatha? Didn't she too serve? Though I don't know in what capacity. Mammie never told me. Didn't she die of leukaemia, a disease kept secret from me when I was a child?

Didn't my Mammie serve as well? And look what happened to her. A great sadness wafts over me. Nano still not a saint, Mammie dead, my best friends dead from AIDS. And here I am trying to make sense of it all, much as I did when Mammie died. I think back to how I handled her death. How I lied trying to glamorise it.

I told everyone that she was killed in front of Tiffany's on 5th Avenue. I even lied to Geoffrey. I didn't tell him the truth until recently. I couldn't bear to imagine Mammie dead on some side street in Astoria by the gas tanks.

Oh Alice M'rie, more's the pity. Sitting there, wiping your nose on your sleeve and boo-hooing for your Mammie and Nano, forgotten by all but yourself.

The bells of St Anne – Shandon Bells – signal midday. With a quick look back at the graves, I head to the English Market. I stroll around, gazing in wonder at the bounty of food. It's all so *now*, so healthy, so exotic. Mr Bell's sells every ingredient I'd want to make a curry. There's not a fry to be had. I stand at a little bar, bearing the unlikely name of Iago, and down a plate of freshly made pasta slathered with pesto and a glass of white wine.

'Arrah, greasy guinea food,' Carey'd say.

'Wrong!' I'd say. 'This is "new" Ireland and we do eat spaghetti.'

'Feast your eyes, girl, feast your eyes,' says master fishmonger Pat O'Connell, as he guts me a fresh grey sole. 'And where's himself?' I love when Geoffrey is referred to as 'himself'.

I pause at the orange-green-blue enamel fountain that's been spurting away since Victoria was Queen, and I can see Mammie, a savoy cabbage in her hand. In Carrigeen, it was a big deal to take a day with Bob at the wheel, and go up to Cork. Now I call Cork my city.

The smell of hops coming from Beamish & Crawford perfumes the air as I cross the Lee on the Nano Nagle Bridge for another look at her grave. You know, I've never visited my Mammie's.

Once again, I sit and look at the hundred white headstones being slowly whittled away in the damp. I think of all the ashes of all the men Geoffrey and I tossed into the Atlantic because they were deprived of traditional burial. Families were so ashamed their son died of AIDS they hid it, leaving their son's friends to memorialise him.

How we trooped down the beach, sometimes in a group, sometimes just Geoffrey and me, holding a small white box heavy with the remains of a friend. How we'd swim way out beyond the breakers to empty it into the ocean. And how sad it became when I realised that swimming in the ocean wasn't *just* swimming any more. It was swimming with the dead.

Yet ocean waters aren't a proper place to mourn a friend. Maybe these nuns are right, being buried here in the heart of the city for the likes of me to sit and ponder.

Ultimately, I hire a Clonakilty genealogist to see if I'm related to Nano. But I'm not. Nano Nagle is not my distant cousin. My eighteenth- and nineteenth-century Slattery and Nagle cousins were spinsters or farmers and, of course, I feel cheated. Yet if delusions of grandeur are inherited, I'm still hoping I might be related to Nano.

17

Diana

I'm alone a lot because Geoffrey's business keeps him in New York or travelling in other countries. Sometimes I'm afraid. Sophie's murder remains unsolved. Yet I don't let fear stop me. Every day when I hitch to Bantry I have interesting conversations with kind strangers, including the murder suspect.

I knew who he was as soon as the car stopped. It was Friday Fair Day and he was going, as was I, into Bantry hoping for an antique 'find'.

I told him I had recently found a pair of Georgian candlesticks and he said he'd found a candlesnuffer. We moved on to painters, Francis Bacon in particular, of whom he had great knowledge and who is a favourite of mine. At Bantry we wished each other good luck. And that was that.

'But weren't you afraid?' I'm asked when I tell of what happened. I wasn't. Still and all, I've had a few frights.

* * *

I'm dead out in the bed with Thomasina when I hear the thunder of hooves. She sits up and, taking my cue from her, I do too. It's a pitch-black night. Yet I'm afraid to put on the light, lest I draw attention to the house and myself. I hear the hooves thunder up the laneway. The nearer they get the more paralysed I become.

For a second I think it's Sophie's murderer, whoever he or she is, come to get me, another female living alone up a long, lonely laneway. When suddenly, the noise stops, reverses and thunders away. Motorcycles.

I call Geoffrey, but he's not home yet. If this happened to Sheila Keating she'd make a cup of tea and forget about it. But this would never happen to Sheila because she's never alone. Instead I take a small whiskey, and give Thomasina an offering of Sheba.

Sitting at the kitchen table, I make a decision then and there to protect myself from bikers, marauders, Sophie's murderer, the Black & Tans, the Provos, the IRA, randy farmers, paedophile priests, skinheads, salesmen, tinkers, tailors, soldiers and sailors.

After rattling this around in my brain for a bit, I realise what most likely stopped the bikers was the cow gate. Now I must make sure no one can open it.

Flashlight in hand, I gird my loins and go outside for a look. The night is still. The air is sweet. I have nothing on hand to block the cow gate but a wheelbarrow that I start filling with sods, branches and stones. I wheel it softly down to the gate, trying to keep 'the Girls' (as I call the cows) from bellowing. They know me. They like me. I hear them moving towards me through the pasture.

I open the gate to wheel the barrow to the opposite side, and I place it strategically so the gate cannot be opened. But when I try and re-enter I can't. I've succeeded in shutting myself out; and I hear the Girls hovering.

The only way I can get over to my side is to climb over the gate. Then I can go home – *Home*, Alice M'rie.

And I do. By dawn's early light, with my nightdress knotted up around my thighs, I climb up and over the cow gate.

Sheila tells me that over the years, summer bikers have used the Big House as an impromptu campsite. Maybe they'll come back. This scares the daylights out of me. So

I buy a thick chain with a sturdy padlock to lock myself away at night from unknown devils.

* * *

Spring has turned into summer and it's 8.15 a.m. on a rainy Sunday. Coffee is perking, tea is in the pot, soda bread is being sliced. By 3 p.m. the place will be packed with neighbours and friends, all set to raise a glass and christen the stable 'Faileth Not'.

I turn on RTÉ Radio 1 for the news. 'Diana, Princess of Wales' – we pay no attention – 'was killed in a car accident ...' Morning silence cracks. 'No, no, no, no!' I wail. 'It's not fair! It's not fair! She can't die.'

Our guests, New York theatre pals John and Larry, stare into their oatmeal. No scenes, please, no scenes. I can read it on their foreheads. I can't blame them. They're on holiday.

I'm caressing a delicate china cup bursting with English roses that was given to Geoffrey and me as a wedding gift. I want to dash it on the ground to ease my rage. But I don't. I can't. I can't make a scene. I can't break a cup I love because a woman I admire has been killed.

RTÉ repeats the bulletin over and over again. Princess Diana ... was killed. Was killed. Was killed in Paris, with her companion, Dodi Fayed. Diana of the Hunt trapped under the Seine in the middle of the night running from paparazzi.

Geoffrey turns on the TV. Every station is running the same black-and-white security footage of Dodi and Diana leaving the Ritz through a revolving door.

I start screaming again, 'It's not fair, it's not fair.' I exchange my cup for an ordinary one, suitable for breaking. Yet I don't dash it to the floor. Can't disgrace myself in front of John and Larry. And a full Irish breakfast, right down to the black pudding, is dished up in silence.

John and Larry tuck in.

'Got to keep our strength up for the day,' says Larry.

Strength indeed! Strength to put up with a wailing woman. My violent reaction surprises me. Even in a darkened cinema, when everyone around me is crying because Dorothy wants to go home to Kansas, I hold it in. I never lose my dignity. I stiff-upper-lip it. That's what Mammie would do, and that's what she'd want from me now.

The phone starts ringing. New York calling – do you *know* anything different? Maybe it's all a mistake. You know how the French are. Outside, the pathetic fallacy weeps upon the flagstones and I worry the party will be rained out.

On Fire Island cocktail parties would be cancelled in favour for mourning tributes in Diana's honour. Everyone would don black armbands. House flags would fly at half mast. But here, because of distance, some people have already started out driving to be with us today.

Killed. Just like that. Just like my Mammie. Killed by a car. My Mammie left there on the street like a bag of garbage. Two women, alike in dignity, crushed upon impact: Diana in white linen, Mammie in a tan raincoat.

RTÉ speaks with the voice of authority. 'We have no further details.'

The TV continues to run the security footage. 'It's not fair, it's not fair, it's not fair,' I scream again. Geoffrey turns off the TV and puts on Sinatra.

Only the day before, in a mysterious piece of syn-chronicity, I inadvertently prepared myself to mourn by purchasing a pair of Victorian jet mourning earrings.

'O yes,' purred Tim, the antique-shop owner. 'Customers have been looking at these earrings all summer, but no one has had the style to buy them but you.' Here I was thinking them merely pretty – that they'd go well with Mammie's linen dress I'm planning to wear at the party. Now I'll wear them to mourn Diana.

Party time approaches. The weather clears up. RTÉ is back on. Prince Charles is leaving for Paris. John and

Larry drive to Field's in Skibbereen to pick up the cake. I poach a salmon, wash wine glasses, slice lemons, set up tea trays and try, but can't, to get Mammie out of my head.

That I'll be wearing a dress Carey missed in his auto-da-fé the afternoon of her death. Years later after he died, I found a 1930s hand-stitched linen yellow shift dress rolled in a ball in the back of her closet.

It's puzzling. Did Mammie stitch the dress herself? Had she a hidden talent for sewing? A talent she found too Irish, too poor, too countrified to reveal? Yet she darned socks, hemmed skirts and taught me to do the same.

With each wine glass I wash, I fixate on the dress and the earrings – proper mourning attire to salute two women who died impeccably dressed.

The weather clears and by 4 p.m., the stable is packed with people all wanting to be here, yet under the circumstances, even feeling a little strange, they're having a good time.

Random comments are bandied about. Oh, it's just as well. She never could have married him. Look how the Royals treated Princess Margaret *and* the Duchess of Windsor.

Sallie asks had I watched Diana's wedding on TV? I hadn't. The day Diana married Charles, Geoffrey and I were walking around Venice, about to embark on our own romance.

After the salmon and before the cake, we salute everyone who helped us create this house, especially Thomasina who, in honour of the event, proceeds to chase cows around in a neighbouring field.

I neither eat nor drink. I miss my mother. As soon as everyone leaves I reach for a whiskey to ease my pain. But Geoffrey stills my hand.

'You can do what you want to, but … '

Geoffrey's a great one for 'buts'. So I sit, looking down the lane to the mountains that separate Cork from Kerry. And I start playing 'Penny Lane' in my head, just like I did at her funeral.

18

Two Women Alike in Dignity

ℒ

Later in the evening, as I scrape a few smidgens of icing from the cake box with my finger, Prince Charles' plane touches down in Paris and Geoffrey puts a moratorium on watching any more of the proceedings on TV. Only then does a sense of calm settle over 'Faileth Not' on this bittersweet August evening.

We drive into Bantry with John and Larry for an evening walk around the bay. In New York our differences would not be so apparent. But in contrast to locals, I realise what an eclectic mix we are as couples: Geoffrey and I – straight, Protestant and Catholic. John and Larry – gay, Mormon and Jew. Yet here we are walking around on this hay-scented evening – four unique people in harmony with the world and each other.

Larry asks me about growing up in Astoria. And I tell him that the first people I ever recognised as different from the Irish Careys were Jewish – our butchers and the Kleins, our downstairs neighbours.

* * *

I'm about ten. I'm down in the landlord's yard looking up at the window of our new neighbours who are immigrants. Leah is making soup. Morris is leaning out the window smoking. Eva, their six-year-old daughter, is trotting downstairs for the English lesson I'm about to give her. *Jane Eyre* was a bit too advanced, so I've found something better in the library.

I'm sitting under my lovely cherry tree. Carey's asleep on the couch, Mammie's banging chops into the frying pan. And Leah leans her large bosom over the windowsill.

'Eva ...' somethingsomethingsomething Jewish ... 'don't *somethingsomething* bother Aleeze.'

'No, no. It's no bother at all, Mrs Klein. I love teaching Eva to read. And I've just the book to do the trick – *Pegeen of Bantry Bay.*'

Carey's baldy head appears in the window.

'Arrah Alice M'rie, what do ye want to know about Bantry Bay?'

'D ... tea?' calls Mammie.

Carey retreats.

Eva pops out the screen door, followed by Leah who is holding a plate of little jelly cookies delicately sprinkled with powder sugar. I say nothing. I don't want my high-pitch brogue to disturb the serenity of this summer afternoon, beneath my beautiful cherry tree on this book-filled day.

Mrs Klein stands to the side holding the plate and I say, 'Eva, I found a new book for you. It's called *Pegeen of Bantry Bay.*'

'Is nice?'

'It's very nice.'

Eva takes a cookie from the plate and eats it with such dainty bites, I want to grab the rest and cram them into my mouth.

'Eva,' says Mrs Klein, 'pil-eeze read to Morr-ees and me.'

Knowing Eva can't read yet, I take the book from her. 'First me. Then you. Okay?'

'Okey-dokey.'

'Once upon a time, long, long ago in old Ireland, there was a girl named Pegeen who lived by Bantry Bay.'

Eva takes the book and turns to her mother who has joined Morris in a cigarette

'Once was a girl.'

'Brava!' screams her mother.

Carey comes down with the garbage.

'Arrah, Missus, Alice M'rie's wasting yer time with all that Irish stuff. This is America, right, land of the free, home of the brave? She should be readin' *Gone With The Wind* or something like that.'

The next day, Mammie and I are shining Miss D.'s stair guards with Brasso.

'Mammie, where's Bantry Bay?'

'Cork.'

'Is that near *Home*?'

'Alice M'rie, why are you reading old stuff like that?'

'It's nice. It's about stuff I don't know. Pegeen lives in a thatched house up in the hills with no electricity or water.'

'Alice M'rie, ye don't need to know about that.'

Next day I make sure Mammie sees me reading *A Tree Grows In Brooklyn*.

I go back to the library, renew my favourite new book and take out *Gone With The Wind* that I put on the coffee table. Carey doesn't even notice it. I secretly read *Pegeen* in bed at night, because I'm dying to know all about 'old' Ireland.

'Mammie, did you ever cook a fresh-killed goose on Michaelmas?'

That was the last straw.

'Alice M'rie, I don't want ye wasting time reading stuff like that. That stuff happened long ago. No one lives that way in Ireland today.'

I quickly return *Pegeen* to the library.

* * *

During Princess Diana's funeral in Westminster Abbey I plant a peach-coloured rose in her honour. As I'm kneeling in the border garden, preparing the soil, I'm watching Prime Minister Tony Blair read from the First Epistle of St Paul to the Corinthians. To my surprise, 'Faileth Not' is interpolated from this Epistle.

Blair reads: '*If I speak with the tongues of men, and of angels, and have not charity, I am become as sounding brass, or a tinkling cymbal.*'

As he continues speaking, I dig into the Irish soil to plant an English rose.

'*Charity suffereth long, and is kind.*'

The day is hot. My hair keeps falling in my face. I keep brushing it away with muddy hands that only serve to smear dirt around. I'm crying, not so much for my Mammie or Diana, but for my old self – that girl who wore a peach-coloured coat to her Mammie's funeral.

'*Charity ... beareth all things, believeth all things, hopeth all things, endureth all things ...*'

It's hard to concentrate with the heat and the midges. Once again I wonder why I care so much for this woman who was not only a princess, but also a media phenomenon. Yet here I am crying my eyes out, focusing on every moment of her funeral while I was barely present at my own mother's.

Blair continues. '*Charity never faileth … when I was a child, I spake as a child, I understood as a child, I thought as a child: but when I became a man, I put away childish things.*'

Childish things … like following a dream of buying a house in Ireland. Dreams, bitter and sweet, that change can bring up. I try to stay in the moment and not have my mind flash to Fire Island wondering what's happening there. I have yet to loose myself from it. It's more real to me than here. Content I am not – at least not yet. Change rattles the bars of memory and I start worrying about what will happen to me, to Geoffrey and to us in the future.

Looking at Diana's boys sitting in Westminster Abbey – so proper, so sad, so young – I think back to Mammie and me seeing the Broadway musical, *Peter Pan*. How I'd play the album in my bedroom over and over again. How I loved singing along to 'I Won't Grow Up', the song Peter sings with the Lost Boys. How I loved singing 'growing up is *awfuller* than all the awful things that ever were'.

How Dave Slattery played it that last night in Carrigeen. And how one night when I was little I must have had a bad dream, and woke up in a panic screaming.

Mammie came in and sat on my bed. I was sort of crying and embarrassed for doing so in a family where crying was frowned upon.

'Mammie, I'm afraid to grow up ... you know, like the song.'

'I know,' she said. And we sat in silence. 'I know.'

I get it now.

* * *

Light is fading to orange over Bantry Bay. Locals are out for their evening stroll – ladies with corgis, teens with blue hair, New Age travellers in dreadlocks, young women in pastel tracksuits swinging their arms on power walks.

Road signs point to Kerry, so near and yet so far. Geoffrey's down at Bantry House buying sunflowers, when suddenly up ahead, I see a woman with a familiar strut walking by the bay.

Something about her gait, her stride, her hat, the cock of her head, makes me think of Mammie. I quicken my pace.

'Mammie ...'

She doesn't hear me.

Yet from the cut of her, she looks just like my mother. A kid shoots me a look. Maybe I said 'Mammie' out loud.

To get a better look I start to trot, to run, to get nearer. It is Mammie. She's walking a dog and wearing a new hat – a green one with feathers. Green. Not black. Not like her.

'Alice M'rie, wear black in winter, white in summer. Nothing else will do.' That's what she used to say.

'Mammie, Mammie ...' I dash up behind her. 'It's me, Alice M'rie.'

She doesn't turn around. Nor is there a bark of recognition from Chindu, Miss D.'s dog. I'm positive it's her. I can tell by her size and the tilt of her head.

'Mammie, Mammie ... it's me. It's me.' She turns around. 'What're you doing here?'

'Alice M'rie, what're ye doing here?'

'I'm living here, by Bantry Bay. Bantry Bay? Remember?'

She doesn't seem to. And her look of disapproval descends from my hennaed hair to my Doc Martens.

'Alice M'rie, why are ye wearing men's shoes and dying your hair?'

I don't reply. Then she says, 'Chindu and I are having a little stroll around the block.' Mammie must be thinking she's in New York.

St Brendan's tolls six.

We stand there looking at each other, wondering who we've become. There's so much to say, and nothing to say. A ferry is coming into port. Fishermen are stowing their lobster pots for the night. And for a second everything seems normal. But nothing is normal. A lady with a corgi passes by without even noticing my Mammie – oh so elegantly dressed – standing right here on the quay on this lovely evening.

Breaking the silence, she turns to me with a fearsome question. 'Alice M'rie, what are ye doing here in Ireland, when ye never visit my grave?'

'Because you're buried in the Bronx! New Yorkers don't go to the Bronx. Geoffrey and I bought a house here. That's why I'm here.'

'I never thought ye'd marry. And I never thought ye'd come back to here.'

'I figured you weren't keen on me marrying because of Carey. But don't you see where we are? This is Bantry Bay.'

Instead of looking at the bay Mammie continues questioning me.

'Then answer me this. What happened to Carey?'

'You don't know?'

'Alice M'rie, believe you me, where I am we know nothing.'

'He dropped dead after Mass.'

A tiny sliver of a smile crosses Mammie's mouth. 'He would, wouldn't he? Always stealing the spotlight. Like him barking in the street.'

The memory of Carey barking at strangers makes me smile a grim little smile, and I continue.

'It was in October, a Saturday evening. Geoffrey and I were on the island. A priest from the Mac called and said Carey was dead. He said Carey had gone to the "five" Mass and as he was leaving the church, he collapsed on the steps and died. The priest found my number in Carey's wallet.

'There was no way Geoffrey and I could get back to the city because the last ferry had already left. I called O'Shea's to make arrangements. At the time I was sick with a strange disease that made it hard for me to walk … do you know about that?'

'Alice M'rie, the beauty of this place is that they tell ye nothing. And we want to know nothing. Now tell me, did ye give Carey a big send-off? Mine was a little skimpy.'

'That was Carey's doing.'

Passersby are noticing me talking into thin air and I'm embarrassed. I sit on a bench and motion for Mammie to do the same. She does and I start telling this woman, whom I think is my mother, about Carey's wake.

'O'Shea put him in the big room. It was packed to the

gills with everyone, everyone, calling him the Great D.D. It drove me mad. The Boston Careys sent down one of those huge bleeding hearts. But instead of real red roses, it was made with green Kleenexes scrunched into green roses, shaped into a shamrock.'

'How did he look?'

'He looked like Carey – Carey in his brown suit. Everyone stood around saying the Great D.D. looked great.

'Geoffrey had never been to an *Irish* wake before and didn't know what he should do. So he just stood there watching everyone shaking my hand and saying, "Sorry for your trouble." Me saying, "It's all right." And them finishing up with, "Your daddy's up in heaven with your mammy." I hated them for it. Wherever you are, I hope Carey isn't.'

Mammie looks away. I shouldn't have let into her like that. Yet she asked what happened and I told her.

I'm embarrassed. I turn and look towards Bantry House hoping to get a glimpse of Geoffrey. I don't. Were he here he could tell me if I was *really* seeing my mother, or imagining her.

With not much more to be said about Carey or his wake, Mammie looks over at the Kerry Mountains. Chindu is gone. I get up and look around for him, but he's nowhere to be seen. So I walk on a bit and Mammie joins me.

'Alice M'rie, listen here to me. I don't know where I've wound up. We don't have a name for it. All I know is that everything everywhere is pretty. There are tons of people walking around and walking around. Once in a while I run into Mitzi, even the General in that uniform of his – the whole megillah. I tell you, 'twas he got to the bottom of it. The day Carey ... you know.'

'I know.'

'Where's Miss D.?'

'Still on 55th Street.'

'How does she look?'

'Older, but OK. She's on TV occasionally.'

Mammie continues. 'The odd celebrity is around as well. Marilyn Monroe. Remember us looking at her through the porthole in Miss D.'s kitchen door?'

We walked as far as the graveyard and I felt I had to speak up. 'Permit me a slight correction. I have seen your grave. I buried Carey right next to you.'

'Then tell me, is it nice?'

'Mammie, it's the Bronx.'

She smiles a wry little smile. There's still a bit of the New Yorker in her.

As we start walking back to the Square questions pop

into my head. 'Mammie, do you remember that library book I tried to teach Eva Klein to read, called *Pegeen of Bantry Bay*? How upset you were when you saw me read it? You said you didn't want me to read it because it was about *old* Ireland.'

Then, quite unbidden, I start to recite.

'"Once upon a time long, long ago in old Ireland there was a girl named Pegeen who lived by Bantry Bay." Do you remember that?'

'No.'

Up on the Square, strings of coloured lights left over from the bazaar have come on.

'Alice M'rie, look … they remind me of …'

'The last time I saw you …'

'At Rockefeller Center's Christmas tree.'

'Afterwards you came down to my flat.'

'I didn't want that for you.' She looks away, embarrassed. 'One small room in the Village. I couldn't bear it.'

'Mammie, listen to me … please. I'm afraid you're going to disappear on me. I know you didn't like where I lived then, and you say you don't like where I am now. Why?'

'Alice M'rie, do ye really think I'd come down to Bantry to tell ye I don't like what y'r doing?'

'Then tell me why did you hate that book?'

'I wanted ye to read about grandeur. It was bad enough we had to live in that freezing flat with Carey. I wanted ye to have something to aspire to. But ye insisted on reading about poor people in Ireland long ago.'

'It was only a book.'

'That's all it takes. Listen to me now. This is not the Ireland I ran from. This is the *new* Ireland. I hear there are supermarkets selling wine. No one drank wine years ago. And no one lives in mud-walled cabins today. People have money to burn. Women can get divorced.

'I was born too soon. I ran from all the stuff you write about. I ran away with Carey, and it never did get better. I didn't want ye to know a thing about *old* Ireland. All I wanted was for ye to be a New Yorker.'

'And I am, Mammie, I am. I am a real New Yorker living in Ireland.'

As if on cue, O'Brien's starts playing the theme from *The Quiet Man*. And as if by magic, Mammie looks both wondrous and different.

'Alice M'rie, ye're back in Ireland. I can't get over it. Ye've come *Home*. Haven't ye?'

'Mammie, I'm not Alice M'rie any more.'

'But ye are, girl. Ye are to me.'

And she disappears.

19

Burying the Animals

We sold 'Magic Flute'. Before we left, we buried the animals down by the moss path.

It's the weekend before Halloween. Geoffrey is taking down Scott's oak panelling and I'm going through the 'summer bedroom' trying to figure out what to do with all the stuff we can't take to Ireland.

A burglar partially solved my problem. Someone broke in, camped out and made a mess – someone who divested me of my sillies and pretties.

But what would I do with sillies and pretties in Ireland, gowns and boas suitable only for gala parties and benefits? What could I possibly do with a manqué First Communion dress and veil I wore to the 'Veil' party? Or

oversized Navy whites I wore to a 'Stage Door Canteen'?
Stuff suitable for a costume box that I'll soon be too old
to wear.

As stuff gets packed up I strive to keep the house
beautiful. Bunches of blue Michaelmas daisies stand on a
Deco sideboard. Late autumn roses, culled from gardens
of closed-for-the-season-houses, perfume the Hoosier
cabinet bought in Delaware that's coming to Ireland for
towels and stuff.

'Magic Flute' glows with candles and oil lamps. But
with all the books and bric-à-brac packed, the light falls
flat.

We've so much stuff … stuff firmly rooted right here. I
could open a shop with all the cookbooks I have, like the
seven Lee Baileys, unknown in Ireland but dear to me.
How can we not take them with us? I read the inscription
Geoffrey wrote to me in *Country Weekends*. '*I bought
this for your Bloomsday Birthday several years ago. It's
now December 1986. Perhaps I waited to inscribe it until
we had a house of our own to have country weekends in.*'

Little did we know then how time changes everything.

Most of our stuff will be out of place in Ireland.
Stuff I'm laying out on the old chrome yellow bed in the
summer bedroom. Stuff we'll leave for the women who've
bought 'Magic Flute'.

The animals are here as well – the ragtag lot looking at me – Dimitri, a pink Easter bunny that sat too long in a Bleecker Street shop window. Snoopy, his ears ripped off by cats, and Sweeney, the golliwog from Liverpool – a present from Father Bob. He, too, nipped by cats.

But it's Tiddly who speaks. Tiddly, who, Mammie claimed, was my first toy. Loved so much over the years, he's now but a small mound of cotton batting wrapped in a red silk scarf. Tiddly, whom I slept with as a child and squeezed to death every night after Mammie died.

'My dear, it's time. We've served you well. Isn't it time you let us go?'

In my mind's eye I can see Tiddly as a small, red-checquered gingham dog. I don't know why he was named Tiddly.

Hurry up, please. It's time.

I pull stuff out of drawers and pile it on the bed: golden dance shoes worn in *Candide*. A cracked pair of spectator pumps, scratched reading glasses, single earrings, pins without clasps.

On a kitchen counter is a line-up of cracked crockery. Stuff. Stuff you keep because you loved the giver. A brown teapot with painted yellow roses, its spout cracked – a gift from our neighbour Cecil, now in a nursing home.

In the shed, muddy boots, work shirts, ski sweaters left by our neighbour, Eric. Stuff given to Geoffrey after Eric died of AIDS. Proud Eric who told not a soul he was dying.

Geoffrey and I wander around outside. Down in the dell is a moss path we cultivated for ten years. When we first bought 'Magic Flute' it was but a small patch of green, and like us, it grew.

The path leads to a patch of ferns and Siberian Iris, where we've interred the ashes of our AIDS guys who didn't want to be cast into the sea.

A few friends would gather, a small ceremony, a song and a sprinkle of whiskey. In the circle where the guys are buried, nothing grows.

'We can't dig 'em up and take 'em with us, can we?'

'And they don't want to go.'

We laugh a little at the Sisyphean task of it. Then I say, 'Let's bury the animals and stuff.'

Near sunset we return to the moss path to bury parts of ourselves to leave here on this island. Geoffrey digs a large hole in a patch of swampy land by the guys, while I line up our talismans.

Eric's stuff goes in first. His work boots provide a foundation, then his ski sweater and cap, Janie's tangerine shoes and my gold ones, Father Bob's clerical collar, an old apron of Mammie's, a cat's food bowl, Geoffrey's workout shirt, his business card and one of my Bakelite bracelets.

Lastly the animals: Snoopy holding on to Tiddly, Dmitri hugging Sweeney.

Hurry up please. It's time.

The light shimmers. A ferry whistle sounds on the bay. A deer nonchalantly strolls by on the boardwalk as we stare at our pile of stuff. I have to smile. The guys would be laughing at us.

Haven't you two anything better to do? Go have a cocktail.

Stuff. They're right of course. I sprinkle some whiskey on the lot and we stare at it. Stuff. Stuff from our life here on this island. Then Geoffrey and I hold onto each other for dear life and cry.

At sunset, we take our last walk on the beach.

We stand looking at the harvest sun as it settles smack over the Atlantic. Down a-ways we see a young couple with a dog and a small rubber boat, also watching. Odd, us gazing at the sun literally setting on this part of our lives, whilst a younger couple unsentimentally pull their boat up on shore, their dog leading the way.

It starts to rain. We head back. As we sit on the couch with wine we hear a skirmish on the kitchen deck. A deer might be there. But it's our neighbour David, with his consort, Cherry Grove's reigning Queen, Timothea, out trick-or-treating, albeit a little early.

What a miraculous sight is this duo, all decked up as jellyfish, shimmering in an autumn rain. Yards of sea-green Mylar drape their heads. Platform shoes make them giants. Tiny concealed flashlights cast light on their tentacles, the ribs of which are umbrellas.

'Trick-or-treat. Trick-or-treat …'

'Oh yes, oh yes,' I hoot. 'I have a real treat here: A Cadbury chocolate bar all the way from Shannon Airport.'

Farewell, we say, waving them down the boardwalk in the rain.

Farewell!

The old Grove spirit bids us goodbye.

The old Grove spirit bids us goodbye.

20

The Spirits

We're in 'Faileth Not' having our morning tea. It's Halloween. We're listening to an old duffer on *Morning Ireland* lay on the palaver about ghosts. Halloween, he says, is a Celtic feast and the beginning of spring in the underworld. While earth is bracing itself for the coming of winter, the spirits below are hot to trot.

People should, indeed must, welcome the dead into their homes by putting lit candles in the windows, and keeping fires banked all night.

Geoffrey and I lock eyes. I see it in his. He sees it in mine. We're thinking of 'Magic Flute'. How we walked out the door for the last time only a week ago. The rain lashing our faces, as we tried wiping away tears while stumbling down the boardwalk for the last time, on our way to the ferry.

Tonight we will celebrate our first Halloween in Ireland. Tonight we will light all the windows in the Big House to welcome back its ghosts in hopes this ritual will give us courage to start restoration.

We spend the day cleaning out the West Room, still full of paint tins, brushes, insulation and moving boxes. Geoffrey squashes empty boxes so damp they collapse like deflated pastry dough while I stomp around on bubble wrap making it go *pop pop pop*.

In the mess, we find an unopened box of stuff shipped over earlier in the year. It wasn't laziness that kept us from opening it, rather the fear of sadness from seeing *stuff* that once meant so much to us.

Inside are black bin bags filled with Grove memorabilia along with six brass candlesticks that lit our dinners there. Tonight we'll place the lit candles in the windows to welcome the spirits.

It's 3 p.m. Night is already drawing in. I start riffling around in the bags filled with paper, much of it damp. It smells of the beach.

Ferry schedules, copies of the *Fire Island News*, party invitations, programmes of benefits and posters of plays and musicals. Musical shows I performed in. *Blithe Spirit, Candide, Damn Yankees* and *The Boy Friend*. Stuff. Stuff we start propping up on the kitchen mantelpiece.

Soon the entire mantelpiece is filled with our past on another island. It's not so much our childhood bending before us, but our youth.

When we walked out the door of 'Magic Flute' were we not as adventurous as the Shannons walking out of this very house sixty years ago, leaving their Irish life behind to start a new life in England?

Sallie says it was sorrow. When their two little boys died they could bear life here no longer. All the turkeys they raised to sell at the Christmas market died. No one knew why or, if they did, no one said anything. So they left under the cover of dark with the clothes on their backs, leaving everything behind. Tonight we will honour the Shannons and all the dead connected with this house and ourselves.

At 6 p.m. we return with beeswax candles and whiskey to sprinkle on the hearth for the spirits. One by one we light the six candlesticks in each room. West Room, kitchen, box room, bedroom, bedroom, boot room.

The flames stand unwavering in the dark, lighting up this old house in west Cork, a house we've put all our hopes, dreams and money into.

We drive down the laneway to the main road. First towards Bantry to see the lighted house *this* way. Then towards Schull to see the house *that* way!

Faaaaaaaaaabuuulous, we scream into the dark. And

for a moment we're back on Fire Island. For a moment we're not over fifty. For a moment all is as it was. For a moment we're screaming with delight with friends long gone. For a moment we're screaming for the sheer joy of screaming.

Faaaaaaaaabuuuuulous we scream and scream and scream into the dark and all the way back up the laneway.

We stop the car by the cow gate and get out to take a long look. All the leaves have fallen and we can see the house well. It's so beautiful. In the dark it doesn't look old. It doesn't look like a ruin. It looks like a glorious old house.

Behind the lighted windows I can see spirits passing between rooms. Prancing up the stairs. Out to the scullery for the turf, over to the fire to make the tea. The Shannons are ready to step into the future. They'll rise before dawn to get the boat train to Liverpool, the parents in travel clothes, Kathleen, their daughter, giddy with excitement. Their two sons left behind in St James' graveyard.

Mammie is also there. And Carey. For didn't the two of them, Alice Slattery and Denis Carey, sally forth from Ireland and sail to a new life in America? And did they not have me, Alice Marie Carey, born in New York City so I would be an American citizen? And I have returned to live in Ireland.

Rain starts to fall as we enter the front door. Drawn from the warmth of the fire in 'Faileth Not', Thomasina joins us.

We need music and Geoffrey goes down to 'Faileth Not' to get the boom box. By luck we get a bit of classical music. He pours two whiskeys. And for the millionth time we walk through this *big* house, a house we haven't a clue what to do with.

'Geoffrey,' I say, 'we're walking on the same bat shit we did three years ago.'

Oh how the candles gleam as we go from West to box to bed to bed to barn to scullery, oohing and aahing. Yes, this must be what the house looked like a hundred years ago. Look how the candlelight reflects on the stone. Look how it gleams upon the glass.

We'll figure out what to do with it. We'll sleep here, cook here, make love here. Tonight is just the beginning. Tonight we'll waltz with our dreams, and the unfulfilled dreams of the Shannons and Alice Slattery and Denis Carey.

Geoffrey lights a small fire in the West Room. We stand in front of it raising our glasses in tribute to our selves and our dead. I throw a drop on the hearth. We return to 'Faileth Not' to bank that fire and go to sleep.

When we wake up on All Saint's Day neither fire has gone out. The spirits are here to stay.